KiDS OUTDOOR PARTIES

PENNY WARNER

Meadowbrook Press
Distributed by Simon & Schuster
New York

Library of Congress Cataloging-in-Publication Data
Warner, Penny.
 Kids' outdoor parties/Penny Warner.
  p. cm.
 Includes index.
 ISBN 0-88166-333-6 (Meadowbrook)—ISBN 0-689-82575-7 (Simon & Schuster)
 1. Children's parties. 2. Entertaining. I.Title.
GV1205.W374 1999
793.2'1—dc21   98-52195
                 CIP

Editor: Jason Sanford
Proofreader: Nancy Baldrica
Production Manager: Joe Gagne
Production Assistant: Danielle White
Cover Art: Gwen Connelly
Illustrations: Laurel Aiello

© 1999 by Penny Warner

Published by Meadowbrook Press, 5451 Smetana Drive, Minnetonka, MN 55343

www.meadowbrookpress.com

BOOK TRADE DISTRIBUTION by Simon & Schuster, a division of Simon and Schuster, Inc., 1230 Avenue of the Americas, New York, NY 10020

04 03 02 01 00 99 10 9 8 7 6 5 4 3 2 1

Printed in the United States of America

DEDICATION

As always,
to Tom, Matt, and Rebecca

ACKNOWLEDGMENTS

To the students at
Diablo Valley College and Chabot College
who contribute wonderful ideas.

I would like to thank Bruce Lansky,
Liya Lev Oertel, Laurel Aiello, and
my wonderful editor Jason Sanford.

CONTENTS

INTRODUCTION

The great outdoors is the perfect place for hosting a children's party, no matter what the season. There's plenty of open space, lots of natural decorations, and the options for fun are limitless! All you need is a theme—which *Kids' Outdoor Parties* will provide—and your outdoor party will come together like sunshine on a summer day.

In *Kids' Outdoor Parties,* I've provided dozens of party themes with suggestions for everything from the welcome invitations to the good-bye favors. You'll find decorating tips for your outdoor party, games to play, activities to entertain, goodies to eat, themed cakes to slice, and fun variations on every outdoor-party theme. Each theme is complete and ready to go as is or can easily be mixed and matched with games and activities from other parties in order to create your own personalized outdoor event!

If your backyard is too small or inappropriate for a party, you can still do anything in this book—simply "borrow" a friend or neighbor's backyard. You can also set up the fun at a local park or school grounds, or take the kids to a site that's related to your theme—such as a beach for the Wet and Wild party! And if the weather threatens to interrupt the fun, just move the whole party inside!

To make your party a success, try to have some other parents help out. Ask the kids to dress appropriately for the party theme you've chosen, so they can play the games and enjoy the activities. And be sure the play area is safe. You might want to cordon off the party place to keep the kids away from any backyard dangers, such as pets, lawn mowers, and swimming pools.

Now open the doors to the great outdoors and invite the guests: It's time for *Kids' Outdoor Parties!*

PARTIES

A DAY AT THE RACES

Spend a day at the races and let your kids test their luck—or skill—at winning a few challenging relay races. From the Big Foot Relay to the Stuff-It Race, this party offers something fun for everyone. On your mark, get set, go!

INVITATIONS

- Write the party details on small toy batons using permanent felt-tip pens, then hand-deliver the batons or mail them in tubes to your party guests.
- Make your own racing flags using plastic cut into triangular shapes. Write the party details on the flags with a felt-tip pen.
- Draw a large stopwatch on white tag-board for each guest. Replace the clock numbers with the party details then cut out the stopwatch. Write "On your mark, get set, go!" across the front in red and green lettering and mail to your guests.

COSTUMES

- Ask the kids to wear comfortable athletic clothes for the competition.

RACE TRACK CAKE

1. Bake a sheet cake according to package directions and cover it with chocolate frosting.
2. Draw oval lines on the cake with white frosting to form a racetrack.
3. Decorate the cake with small plastic racers and tiny racing flags.

- Make racing shirts for the guests by writing their names and numbers with puffy paints on inexpensive white T-shirts.

DECORATIONS

- Decorate the yard with crepe paper ribbons, streamers, and racing flags. Use yellow ribbon to indicate the start and finish lines. Hang cheering signs on the fence with slogans, such as "Go!," "You can do it!," and "You're a Winner!"

GAMES

- Big Foot Relay: Ask the guests to bring two shoeboxes to the party. Tape the lids onto the boxes, then cut a one-inch-wide and four-inch-long slit in each top.

Have the contestants slip their feet into the slits in the boxes and race.

- Bowlegged Race: Ask each guest to bring a tennis ball, or provide one for each participant. Line the guests up, give them each one ball, and have them hold the ball between their knees. The first kid to race to the finish line without dropping his or her ball wins.
- Foot-to-Foot Race: Have the players line up at the starting line. Tell them they have to race to the finish line by placing one foot directly in front of the other, toe to heel. It'll be a challenge for the players to finish without losing their balance and falling!

- Book Worm Relay: Line up the players and give each of them a book to balance on their heads—without using their hands. Have them race to the finish line. Any player who finishes without dropping the book gets to race again, this time with something more difficult to balance, such as a toy, a small plate, an egg, and so on.
- Paper Chase: Divide players into teams and line them up at the starting line. Give the first players on each team two sheets of newspaper. Each player must race to the finish line—stepping only on the newspaper—then return and pass the newspaper to the next player, who continues racing. The first team to finish wins.
- Pass-the-Hat Relay: Divide the players into teams and line them up. Give the first players on each team a hat and a stick. Have them pass the hat down the line of players, balancing the hat on the stick. If a player touches the hat with his or her hands, or drops the hat, the hat goes back to the beginning of the line and that team must start over. The first team to finish wins.
- Spaghetti Mess: Create a twisting and turning maze using twelve-foot lengths of yarn. (Have one piece of yarn for each pair of kids.) Wind each strand of yarn back and forth, over and under every other piece of yarn until you have a looping mess (try to avoid knotting the yarn). Then give each kid one end of the yarn.

The object of the race is for the kids to wind their way along the yarn until they discover who is also holding on to their yarn. The first pair of kids to reach each other in the middle wins.

- Stuff-It Race: Divide the players into teams of four or five. Select one member from each team to dress up in an over-sized sweatshirt and pants. Have the remaining team members inflate fifty balloons and stuff them into the sweatsuit without popping the balloons. The first team to use up all the balloons wins.

ACTIVITIES

- Divide the kids into teams and have them come up with their own fun relay race to play.

VARIATIONS

- Instead of relay races, have the kids perform a series of stunts, such as balancing acts, ball tasks, jump-rope games, hopscotch variations, or tumbling tricks.

HELPFUL HINTS

- Be sure to have lots of prizes on hand—for both winners and losers. The prizes don't have to be expensive, just fun. Red, white, and blue prize ribbons are a great way to enhance self-esteem.
- Just for fun, have some booby prizes on hand for the losers.

- Snail Race: Collect some garden snails and give one to each guest. Have the guests paint the snail shells with non-toxic poster paint so each kid can recognize his or her snail. Then have the guests mark off a small racetrack on the ground and race their snails.

FOOD

- Serve spaghetti in honor of the Spaghetti Mess and foot-long hot dogs for the Big Foot Relay.
- Provide plenty of bottled water or sports drinks.

FAVORS

- Send guests home with trophies and prize ribbons.
- Give guests racing flags to put on their walls.
- Hand out the tiny toys from the cake.
- Give the guests game books, balls, and balloons to take home.

ARCHEOLOGY EXPEDITION

Explore all the possibilities of fun and games on your Archeology Expedition. All you need is a compass to tell you where to go and a party time machine to get you there!

INVITATIONS

- Draw ancient-looking maps to the party site on cream-colored construction paper. When finished, wrinkle the paper and burn the edges to make it look old. Then roll the maps up, place in tubes, and mail to all the invited archeologists.
- Write your party invitations in made-up hieroglyphics. Include a decoder inside the envelope so the guests can decipher the message.
- Send the kids a toy compass with the party details attached.

COSTUMES

- Ask the guests to come dressed as scientists in white lab coats (large white shirts) or archeologists in khaki shirts—or provide the shirts to the kids as they arrive.
- Have the guests bring any small tools that might be needed at the dig, such as plastic shovels, magnifying glasses, paintbrushes, and so on.

DECORATIONS

- Hang travel posters of the pyramids or other archeological sites on the fence around the party area.

- Build a small pyramid in the backyard, using cardboard if you want it to be kid-sized or Popsicle sticks if you want it to be a centerpiece.
- Provide a supply of archeology tools for the guests to use, such as plastic shovels, compasses, maps, paintbrushes, glue, and so on. Set the tools on the party table as a centerpiece until it's time to use them.

GAMES

- Falling Pyramid: Divide the group into teams. Give each team either a deck of cards, different-sized pieces of cardboard, or Popsicle sticks. The teams then have five to ten minutes to build a pyramid that doesn't fall over. The team with the tallest pyramid wins.
- Fossil Hunt: Buy a bunch of inexpensive plastic insects or dinosaurs. Hide or bury the small toys in the backyard or sandbox. Let the guests collect as many as they can. Let the guests keep what they discover.
- Mystery Maps: Divide the kids into teams and give each team a map that leads to a buried artifact or hidden treasure. Make each map different, with cryptic clues or picture-graphs, and hide the artifacts in different places, so that each team gets to find a treasure. The first team to find their treasure wins.

PYRAMID CAKE

1. Bake a square cake and let cool.
2. Cut the cake in half diagonally to form two triangles.
3. Frost the tops of both triangles and place them together. Turn the cake on its side to form a pyramid.
4. Frost the rest of the cake.
5. Using decorator tubes, add lines around the cake to form ridges.
6. Top the cake with a flag, a toy mummy, or a candle.

ACTIVITIES

- Ancient Petroglyphs: At the stationery store, buy some antique-looking paper. Pick up a book from the library on petroglyphs and hieroglyphs and photocopy the illustrations so the kids can see them easily. Then provide the kids with felt-tip pens—or paint and brushes—and have them make up their own ancient petroglyphs.
- Buy a three-dimensional dinosaur puzzle from a science or nature store, and have the kids assemble it to recreate a dinosaur fossil.

them in small individual plastic bags to make "sand." Add a tablespoon or two of chocolate sprinkles to make "ants." Mix well and give a bag to each archeologist.

- Make Mummified Dates by cutting open dates and removing the pits. Fill with cream cheese or peanut butter, and close back up. Serve to the hungry archeologists. For added fun, stick a gummy insect inside.
- Sprinkle the party table with gummy insects, worms, spiders, and other yucky but edible finds and let the kids gobble them up.

FAVORS

- Send the guests home with archeology tools, compasses, and all the goodies they have dug up.
- Give each guest a bag of Ants-in-the-Sand to take home.
- Give the kids small dinosaur puzzles to put together when they get home.

VARIATIONS

- Take the kids to the park so they have a larger area to explore.
- Make a trip to a local museum that houses mummies and other archeological finds.

HELPFUL HINTS

- Be sure to hide lots of little toys so that everyone finds something while on the expedition.

- King Tut-Tut: Have the kids create their own mummies using toilet paper, crepe paper, or torn strips of fabric. Divide the guests into groups and select one kid from each team to be the "mummy." Have the teams wrap their mummies in creative ways, then decorate the mummies using felt-tip pens. Award a prize for the most creative, the ugliest, the scariest, the cutest, and so on.

FOOD

- Serve Ants-in-the-Sand. Crush four to six graham crackers per guest and place

BACKYARD BOWLING

The kids will be bowled over by this Backyard Bowling party—and they won't even need real bowling balls! Any ball will do, as long as the kids have something fun to knock over. Get ready for a striking good time!

INVITATIONS

- To make bowling ball invitations, fold sheets of black construction paper in half and cut out circles. Be sure not to cut the edge of the circle where the paper is folded; this will hold the two parts of the card together. Decorate the tops of the round cards with three small white circles. Open the cards and write the party details inside using white or silver ink.
- Cut out several bowling pins from white construction paper. Draw stripes on the necks of the pins using a felt-tip pen. Write a few of the party details on one

BOWLING BALL CAKE

1. Bake two chocolate cakes in round pans.
2. Layer the cakes and frost them with light-colored frosting.
3. Draw alleys with black or chocolate tube icing.
4. Top with tiny toy bowling pins (available at bakery shops and toy stores) or small white mints, set up in triangle formation, and malt balls for bowling balls.

pin, more details on the next pin, and so on. Stick the pins in envelopes and mail to the guests. When the guests open the envelopes and pour out the pins, they'll have to piece the information together to figure out what it says.
- Pick up some brochures at your local bowling alley, write the party details inside with a black felt-tip pen, and mail to the guests.

COSTUMES

- Ask the kids to wear funny bowling shirts they've created using puffy paints or felt-tip pens and one of their parent's old shirts. Or provide the shirts, paints, and pens for the kids and let them decorate the shirts at the party.
- Divide the guests into teams, then write each team's name and logo on T-shirts with felt-tip pens or puffy paints. Give the shirts to the kids as they arrive.

DECORATIONS

- Cut out giant bowling balls from black tagboard or construction paper and large pins from white paper. Write the names of the guests on the balls and pins, then mount them on the fence, the side of the house, or on the backyard trees.
- Cut out and personalize construction paper bowling balls for place mats and set them on the party table. Buy some old pins from the local bowling alley to use as decorations on the table. Personalize them and give them as take-home gifts at the end of the party.
- Make a giant scoreboard from poster board and mount it on the fence or wall. Keep score as the players knock down pins during the games.

GAMES

- Batty Bowling: Find a number of silly or odd items that can be knocked over by a ball, such as a plastic milk carton, a candlestick, a stand-up doll, a plastic vase of flowers, a pizza box, a tower of empty cans, an umbrella stand, an empty oatmeal container, and a book. Line them up like bowling pins and let the bowlers try to knock them over with volleyballs, tennis balls, or golf balls.
- Line Bowling: Instead of setting up the pins in a triangular pattern, set them up in a long row. Let one player roll a ball to knock over a pin. If the player is successful, let him or her go again. If not, the line is reset and the turn moves to

another player. Whoever knocks them all over, one by one, wins.

- Squirt Gun Bowling: Instead of a bowling ball, use a water gun. Make paper pins by cutting out small white construction paper triangles, folding them into cones, and propping them up on a fence or table. Give each kid five seconds to squirt the pins over, then reset the pins and let the next kid go. Keep score. Whoever has the highest score after five rounds wins.

ACTIVITIES

- Domino Bowling: Buy a bunch of inexpensive dominoes and give equal amounts to all the guests. Have them spread out on the patio or driveway and build a domino track by standing each domino upright close to one another. When everyone's finished, let one kid knock over the first domino as the other guests watch.

VARIATIONS

- Take the kids to a bowling alley and let them play a real game.

HELPFUL HINTS

- Save those squeezable plastic juice bottles—they make great bowling pins.
- Ask the local bowling alley if they have any old equipment they are willing to sell or lend for the party.

- Let the kids make their own pins using white construction paper. Have them decorate the pins with felt-tip pens, puffy paints, glitter, and so on.

FOOD

- Serve classic bowling alley food, such as hot dogs, nachos, and soda.
- Make edible bowling balls and pins using meatballs and tiny wieners, served with a dipping sauce. For dessert, serve malted "bowling" balls and cookies in the shape of pins.

FAVORS

- Let the bowlers keep their bowling shirts.
- Give each kid a personalized bowling pin to take home.
- Buy each guest a little bowling set, available at toy stores.

BALLOON BLAST

It's an all-balloon party at this Balloon Blast. The party begins with balloon invitations, ends with balloon favors—and has billions of balloons in between. All you need is a little hot air!

INVITATIONS

- Blow up a balloon and pinch the end. Write party details on the balloon using a felt-tip pen. Repeat for each guest. Deflate the balloons, insert in envelopes, and mail. The guests will have to blow up the balloons to read the party details.
- Write the party details on small squares of colored paper and roll into thin tubes. Insert tubes into balloons and blow up balloons. Hand deliver or mail in boxes to guests. They'll have to pop the balloons to read the details.
- Buy a helium balloon for each guest and write the party details on a small sheet of paper. Punch a hole in the paper and attach by string to the balloon. Tie balloons to the doorknobs or mailboxes of guests.
- Make balloon invitations from construction paper. Fold paper in half and cut out ovals, being careful not to cut where the paper is folded; this will hold the two parts of the card together. Write the party details inside the cards. Attach a length of string. Mail to guests.

COSTUMES

- Send deflated balloons to the kids via the invitation, and ask them to use the balloons in some creative way as part of their costume. One guest might tie inflated balloons to her shoes, another might make a tie out of deflated balloons, and another might create an interesting balloon hat. Have them wear the balloon accessories to the party and award a prize for the most imaginative costume.

DECORATIONS

- Tie a balloon to every tree, shrub, fence post, and anything else in your yard.
- Use helium balloons tied together to make archways or canopies.
- Make balloon animals and set them on the table as a centerpiece.

GAMES

- Air Balloon: Give each guest a large balloon and have everyone stand in a circle. On the word "Go!" have the guests hit their balloons into the air. Every time a balloon gets near a kid, he or she must hit it into the air again. If a balloon touches the ground, the kid nearest that balloon is out. Award a prize to the last player.

BALLOON CAKE

1. Bake cake batter in a well-greased, round, ovenproof bowl—a little longer than the baking instructions recommend. Insert toothpick to see if the cake is finished; if no batter sticks to the toothpick, the cake is ready.
2. Remove cake from bowl and frost with icing tinted to a favorite color.
3. Write any party details on the cake with frosting tubes. Make a string at the bottom of the cake with frosting or licorice whips.
4. Surround the Balloon Cake with balloon-shaped cupcakes.

- Balloon Bounce: For a variation on Air Balloon, have the players keep the balloons up in the air using only their heads—or feet!
- Balloon Stomp: Blow up a balloon for each player and attach a string. Have players tie the balloons to their left ankles, leaving about a foot of string between the ankle and balloon. On the word "Go!" have the players attempt to pop one another's balloons—without getting their own balloon popped! The last player with an intact balloon wins.
- Balloon Stunts: Write a number of body stunts or tricks on small pieces of paper, such as "Jump on one foot," "Walk backwards," "Do a deep knee-bend," and so on. Have each player draw a piece of paper from a hat and follow the instructions while trying to keep his or her balloon up in the air!

- Cement Shoes: Have the players try to keep their balloons up in the air without moving from the spot where they stand.
- Tennis Balloon: Give the players tennis rackets and have them pair up. Let them bat a balloon back and forth over a net, table, or fence. Players score one point if the balloon hits the ground on their opponent's side of the net.
- Volley Balloon: Divide the group into two teams on either side of a volleyball net. Have them play volleyball with a balloon.

ACTIVITIES
- Let the kids make their own balloon animals. Provide felt-tip pens or face stickers for added detail and decoration.
- Let the kids blow up balloons and draw their own funny faces on them with felt-tip pens. Cut out construction paper feet and attach them to the bottoms of

the balloon faces with double-stick tape. Award prizes for the funniest faces.

FOOD
- Make balloon-shaped snacks, such as cracker sandwiches filled with peanut butter and a thin licorice whip sticking out for the string.
- Make a variety of fruit balls, insert colored toothpicks, and stick the fruit balloons into a Styrofoam block covered with a paper napkin.
- Offer lots of round snacks, such as bowls of Trix cereal, doughnut holes, Skittles, gumballs, meatballs, and so on.

FAVORS
- Send the kids home with the balloon animals and balloon people they made.
- Give the guests a sack of deflated balloons to play with at home.
- Hand each guest a personalized balloon.

VARIATIONS
- Have a Bubble Party instead of a Balloon Party, and make bubble-blowing the theme for your invitations, food, games, and favors.

HELPFUL HINTS
- Balloons can be dangerous so watch the kids as they play. If anyone is afraid of the loud noises when the balloons pop, you might provide ear plugs so they can still enjoy the fun.

BEACH LUAU

Put on your bathing suits, bring your towels, and head on over for a Beach Luau. No need to fly to the islands—you can turn your backyard into a tropical paradise with a little imagination and creativity!

INVITATIONS

- Buy some coconuts at the grocery store and write the party details right on them with a black felt-tip pen. For fun, make a funny face on the coconut first. Hand deliver or mail to guests.
- Make construction paper coconuts by folding sheets of brown paper in half and cutting circles. Do not cut where the paper is folded; this will hold the two parts of the card together. Use a felt pen to add coconut details and a funny face. Place in envelopes with a little bit of sand and tiny, inexpensive shell neck-laces. Mail to guests.

- Collect brochures of the tropics from travel agencies and write party details inside, then mail to guests.

COSTUMES

- Ask the vacationers to come dressed as tacky tourists in Hawaiian shirts and hula skirts, or ask them to wear their bathing suits under regular clothes.

PINEAPPLE UPSIDE-DOWN CAKE

1. Mix cake according to directions.
2. Layer pineapple slices in bottom of sheet cake pan, fill holes with maraschino cherries, and pour in the liquid of canned pineapples.
3. Pour in cake batter and bake accord-ing to package directions.
4. When done, flip cake over onto platter—pineapple side up.
5. Top with tiny paper umbrellas for decoration.

- If you can borrow a surfboard, it makes a great prop.
- Hang tiny shell necklaces around the yard.

GAMES

- Beach Volleyball: Set up a volleyball net or rope in the backyard and divide the players into two teams. Instead of using a volleyball, have the kids play the game with a large beach ball.
- Island Hopping: Cut out "islands" from brown construction paper; make each island about two feet in diameter. Place the islands within stepping distance of one another around the yard, but make each one a stretch. Have the players take turns trying to Island Hop from one island to another, without falling into the ocean to be devoured by sharks. Time the kids to make it exciting, or have a race between two teams.
- Limbo: Hold a long stick or broom handle parallel to the ground, about chest high to the players. Put on some Hawaiian music and have the players try to walk under the stick limbo-style— bending backwards instead of forwards. After everyone has had a turn, keep going, but lower the stick each time you play another round.
- Surf's Up: Borrow a surfboard and set it on the ground. Have one player step up on it while the rest of the players sit around the board and move it in an effort to rock him or her off.

DECORATIONS

- Drape fishnets over the fence and the party table to create a tropical look.
- Hang plastic fish from the fence or the trees. Place extra fish on the table, personalized with each guest's name.
- Light tiki torches or string up colored lights if the party is at night.
- Fill the party area with large paper flowers and lots of tropical fruit, such as coconuts, bananas, papayas, and pineapples.

ACTIVITIES

- Hula-Do: Choose someone to be Hula Simon. Line the guests up in a row and have them respond to orders from Hula Simon, but only when he or she says "Hula-Do." Have all the commands relate to the hula dance. Be sure to make up your own wacky steps.
- Let the kids make shell necklaces by buying kits at the hobby store. Or get them to make candy leis by tying wrapped candies together with decorative ribbon.
- Tropical Sand Storm: Give each guest a small jar, such as a clean baby food jar. Set bowls of fine sand on the table and provide large sticks of sidewalk chalk. Have the kids color the sand by rubbing the chalk over the sand grains in the bowls until they are tinted. Then let them fill their jars with layers of colored sand. Fill the jars to the top, seal them shut with glue, and paint the lids.

VARIATIONS

- Take the kids to the local beach and enjoy your party on real sand.
- Turn the event into a pool party.

HELPFUL HINTS

- Be sure to cover everyone with sun protection lotion before they get too much sun.

FOOD

- Make Fruit Kebab by cutting up tropical fruits—such as bananas, pineapple, and so on—and skewering them onto long toothpicks.
- Create a Pineapple Boat by cutting a pineapple in half and removing the pineapple meat. When clean, fill the boats with chunks of pineapple, banana slices, cherries, and other fruits.
- Offer the kids banana splits for dessert.

FAVORS

- Give the kids shell necklaces and candy leis to wear home.
- Let the guests have their own beach balls.
- Offer everyone a beach kit filled with suntan lotion, inexpensive sunglasses, a water bottle, and a fan.

BIKE TREK

Grab the bikes and gather the gang for a rigorous road rally. Just follow the map, watch for special instructions, and hopefully you'll all meet up at the surprise destination!

INVITATIONS

- Cut out pictures of cool bikes from toy catalogs or from bike shop brochures. Glue them onto the front of three-fold brochure-style paper and write the party details inside.
- Send bike decals to the guests with party details written in permanent felt-tip pen on the backs.
- Tape safety reflector stripes on the envelopes for a hot biker look.

COSTUMES

- Ask the kids to come dressed in loud, colorful biking shorts and tops—the wilder, the better.
- Provide white shirts for the bikers and let the kids decorate them with different colors of reflector tape.
- Provide racing shirts of the same color for all the guests. Buy some iron-on letters and put the kids' last names on the backs of the shirts, along with racing numbers on both both sides.

DECORATIONS

- Provide decorations for the kids so they can brighten up their bikes before the road rally. Include such accessories as colorful reflector tape, decals, handlebar streamers, crepe paper, bells, horns, mini license plates, and sports cards to clip onto the spokes of the wheels.
- Write the bike trek instructions on decorative paper to make it more fun to read.

GAMES

- Racetrack: Set up a racetrack in an empty parking lot, using homemade orange cones made from stiff tagboard to shape the path. Time the kids as they ride through the racetrack. Offer a prize to the one who travels the racetrack in the shortest amount of time.

- Obstacle Course: Set up an obstacle course for the bikes. Let the bikers try to maneuver through the tight paths and twisty turns without dumping their bikes.
- Copycat Bike: Take turns having bikers lead the group on a follow-the-leader run.
- Bike Circus: Let the kids show off their bike tricks. The one who does the most dazzling tricks wins a prize. Have them teach each other the tricks, too.

ACTIVITIES

- Road Rally: Set up a course for players to follow using a map of the local neighborhood or a nearby park. Several days before the event, follow the course on your bike and write down directions for the kids to follow. For example, you might write down, "Turn left at the oak tree," "Follow the path through the tunnel," or "Turn right at the first path." When the bikers arrive, pass out the directions and send them on their way.
- When all the bikers have finished the rally, award prizes in a variety of categories, such as "First Biker to Arrive,"

"Last Biker to Arrive," "Most Exhausted-Looking Biker," "Biker Who Got Lost the Most," "Biker Who Bit the Pavement," and so on.

FOOD

- Provide plastic water bottles for all the bikers, or substitute a popular sports drink. Decorate the bottles with puffy paints and personalize them with the guests' names.
- Send along bags of trail mix for the bike trail, in case the kids need a quick pick-me-up along the route. Or surprise them by setting up a card table with drinks and snacks somewhere on the route.

ROAD RALLY CAKE

1. Bake a sheet cake and cover it with chocolate frosting.
2. Outline a path in white icing to simulate a bike path.
3. Place tiny bicycles along the path, racing toward the finish line.
4. Set a small plastic trophy at the end.

- End the party at a pizza parlor or fast food restaurant and let the kids order what they want.
- At the end of the road rally, provide a picnic with sandwiches, drinks, cookies, and chips.

FAVORS

- When you cut the cake, give the toy trophy to the winner of one of the races.
- Pass out the toy bikes to the rest of the gang.
- Offer the riders accessories for their bikes, such as horns, streamers, decals, mirrors, personalized mini license plates, and so on.

VARIATIONS

- Write the directions on paper plates instead of on sheets of paper. Post the plates along the route so the bikers have to watch for the clues as they travel.
- Write cryptic clues instead of obvious directions and let the bikers decode the messages to follow the correct route. For example, you might write, "Turn left at the next presidential street" (Jefferson Street), or, "Make a U-turn where the cops hang out" (the doughnut shop).

HELPFUL HINTS

- Write or print the directions on clean sheets of paper and number them for clarity.
- Be sure to write down the final destination of the road rally in case some bikers get lost.

BOUNCING BALLS

There isn't a kid on the planet who doesn't enjoy playing with a ball. Large or small, soft or firm, plain or colorful, balls provide hours of entertainment for kids of all ages. Start your party off with a bounce!

INVITATIONS

- Cut out ball shapes from folded construction paper. Do not cut the edges of the balls where the paper is folded; this will hold the two parts of the cards together. Decorate outsides of cards with felt-tip pens, glitter, puffy paints, and stickers. Write party details inside.
- Purchase some small balls and write the party details on them using a permanent felt-tip pen. Place them in boxes and mail to guests.
- Blow up some inexpensive beach balls and write the party details on them

using felt-tip pens. Deflate the balls and mail in large envelopes.

COSTUMES

- Ask the kids to attach balls to themselves in creative ways, such as tied to their shoes, hanging from their belt loops, or worn as part of a hat.
- Suggest the kids dress as favorite sports players.

DECORATIONS

- Cut out giant paper balls from large sheets of construction paper or poster board. Decorate balls to represent dif-

BIG BALL CAKE

1. Mix batter according to package directions.
2. Grease a two or three-quart oven-proof bowl and pour in batter.
3. Bake a little longer than the recommended baking time.
4. Flip cake onto large platter. Sprinkle platter with green-tinted coconut to form the playing field.
5. Frost the cake to look like a favorite type of ball, such as a soccer ball, baseball, beachball, and so on.

ferent sports, such as football, base-ball, soccer, tennis, and golf.

- Hang beach balls along the fence or place them around the yard.
- Make a centerpiece out of balls placed in a large bowl. You might include tennis balls, baseballs, racquetballs, whiffle balls, and so on.
- Make a silly centerpiece using other types of balls, such as popcorn balls, balls of yarn, sock balls, pompom balls, meatballs, and so on.
- Cut out round place mats from construction paper and set them on the table. Personalize each one.

GAMES

- Circle Dodge Ball: Have the players form a circle. Choose one kid to stand in the middle. Give one of the players in the circle a soccer ball and have him or her throw the ball at the player in the middle. If the ball misses, the player who gets the ball on the other side of the circle gets a turn. If the ball hits the player in the middle, that player comes out and the kid who threw the ball gets a turn in the middle.
- Jai Alai: Give each player a small plastic bowl or box. Pair the players up in two rows facing each other, about three feet apart. Give each player in one row a tennis ball. Players must use their container to toss the ball to their partners, while their partners must try to catch the ball in their container. Each time the ball is successfully thrown and caught, move the players farther and farther apart. Any pair that drops their ball is out. Play until only one pair remains.
- Name-It Ball: Have players form a circle. Give one player a rubber ball. That player selects a category, such as "candy bars." He or she then bounces the ball to another player in the circle, who must catch the ball, state an item from the category, such as "Snickers," and keep the ball moving to the next player. If a player can't name an item, holds the ball too long, or repeats an item, he or she is out.

ACTIVITIES

- Blanket Ball: Form a circle with all the kids. Place a blanket or sheet in the middle of the circle; have each kid lift the blanket waist high in the air. Toss a beachball into the center. The kids then try to keep the ball in the air by raising and lowering the blanket— without letting the ball bounce off!
- Pass 'N' Catch: Form a circle. Give each player a different ball. On the word "Go!" all the kids throw their balls across the circle to another kid, while trying to catch a ball coming back.
- Seven-Up: Give one child a rubber ball and have him or her bounce the ball seven times. In between each bounce he or she must do a stunt or trick, such as clap hands, duck down, spin around, and so on.
- Wacky Ball: Give each guest a Ping-Pong ball and have him or her tape a coin to it. Then have the kids try to roll the balls from a starting line to a finish line.

VARIATIONS

- Take them out to a ball game!
- Mix the balls and games—play volleyball with a football, Ping-Pong with a tennis ball, baseball with a soccer ball, and football with a beachball.

HELPFUL HINTS

- Keep a watchful eye so the kids don't get hurt with the balls.

FOOD

- Have the kids make popcorn balls. Tint the syrup a special color for added fun.
- Serve meatballs with toothpicks and dipping sauce.
- Set out cheese balls and round crackers for the hungry ball players.
- Serve balls of ice cream with the cake.
- Give the kids ballpark food—hot dogs, nachos, pretzels, and sodas.

FAVORS

- Give the kids a variety of balls to take home, including a Ping-Pong ball, tennis ball, whiffle ball, beach ball, and a super-bouncing ball.
- Hand out keepsake softballs to all the guests. Have them sign the balls, then pass them on, until all the guests have signed all the balls.

22

CARNIVAL TIME

Your own backyard is the perfect place to host a carnival party. Let the whole family help prepare for the guests by making the booths, planning the games, and buying the favors. It's Carnival Time!

INVITATIONS
- Cut out giant tickets from construction paper, using real tickets as models. Write the party details on the tickets, stuff into large manila envelopes, and mail to guests.
- Buy a roll of tickets from a party store, rip off a half dozen or so for each guest, then write the party details on the tickets. Tear the strips into individual tickets, mix them up, place in envelopes, and mail.
- Insert a small carnival toy—such as a plastic whistle, a fingertrap, or a tiny puzzle—inside the envelopes.

COSTUMES
- Ask the kids to dress like carnival workers.
- Make special carnival shirts using inexpensive T-shirts and puffy paints. Write the guests' names on the backs.

DECORATIONS
- Collect large boxes from appliance stores to use as carnival booths, then paint the boxes with poster paint. Add flowers, stars, and other designs for detail. Set the booths in a semicircle in the yard.
- Decorate the fence, patio, and house with crepe paper streamers to make the area festive. Add balloons to the booths for color and fun.
- Hang posters with carnival slogans on the fence, such as "Guess Your Weight," "Ten Throws for a Dime," and "Win a Prize!"
- Play carnival or marching band music in the background.

GAMES

- **Balloon Pop:** Write the names of different prizes on small pieces of paper and roll them up into little tubes. Blow up enough balloons for all the guests, insert one slip of paper into each balloon, then tie off the balloons. Have the players sit in a circle around the balloons. Blindfold one player and let him or her try to find and pop a balloon by stomping on it. When the balloon pops, remove the blindfold and read the name of the prize. Repeat with all of the kids.
- **Bottle Ring:** For this classic carnival game, set up twelve bottles on a platform, four across by three down. Cut out rings from heavy cardboard, making sure the rings are large enough to easily fit around the necks of the bottles. Let the kids try to toss the rings over the bottlenecks to win prizes.
- **Guess How Many:** Count out a large number of small candies and place

them in a jar. The guest whose guesses the actual number of candies wins the jar and the candy.
- **Nosy the Clown:** Paint one booth to look like a giant clown face. Cut a circle where the nose should be, large enough to toss a beanbag through. Give prizes to the kids who toss the most beanbags through the nose.
- **Penny Toss:** Place a number of empty containers of varying sizes—such as a tuna can, a juice can, and so on—on a platform. Set the cans up in random order, assigning each one a point value based on difficulty. Give the players ten pennies and let the kids try to toss them into the cans. Award different prizes for different point totals.

CAROUSEL CAKE

1. Bake two round layer cakes. Stack them on top of each other. Frost with white icing.
2. Stick peppermint sticks in a circle on the cake to form a carousel.
3. Set tiny toy animals next to the peppermint sticks.
4. Frost a pie pan and set it on top of the peppermint sticks for the roof of the carousel.

kids reach into the Black Hole one at a time and grab a prize.

- Take My Picture: On one of the large boxes, draw a picture of a popular character like Batman, one of the Power Rangers, or Barbie. When you are finished, cut out the character's face. Have the kids stick their faces into the hole and take pictures of their "new look." Use an instant camera for instant party fun, or mail the pictures to the kids later.
- T-shirts: Let the kids make carnival shirts using white T-shirts and puffy paints or decals.

FOOD

- Serve carnival treats, such as popcorn, peanuts, Cracker Jack, and pretzels.
- Make corn dogs on sticks and serve them with corn on the cob.

FAVORS

- The kids should have lots of small prizes to take home.
- Give the kids a goody bag filled with surprises that they can't open until they get home.

- Shooting Gallery: Set up plastic toys along a fence or platform. Line the players opposite the toys, several feet away, and give each kid a water gun. At the word "Go!" have them try to squirt over as many toys as possible. Give prizes to the kids who knock over the most toys.

ACTIVITIES

- Go Fishing: Line up all the kids at the Fishing Pond Booth. Hand the first fisherman a pole and have him or her throw it into the "pond" behind the booth. Tie a prize to the end of the line. Pull up the line and let the kid discover the prize!
- Grab Bag: Paint one of the booths black and call it the Black Hole Booth. Hide wrapped prizes inside the booth. Let the

VARIATIONS

- Invite the kids to help set up the carnival one day, then enjoy it the next day.

HELPFUL HINTS

- Make sure there are lots of prizes for both winners and losers.

CIRCUS PARTY

Come one, come all, to the greatest show on earth—the Circus Party! There will be lots of big top fun and clowning around. So step right up, one and all. The show is about to begin!

INVITATIONS

- Find a picture of a clown in a coloring book and reproduce it for your guests. Glue spongy clown noses—available at party and costume stores—to the faces. Write party details on the backs of the drawings and mail to the guests.
- Draw a circus poster with the party details in the headlines and in the small print. Add a picture of the guest of honor with a clown nose attached. Mail to the guests.
- Buy a package of tiny plastic circus animals or clowns, attach a note with the party details to each toy, and mail in small boxes to the guest.

CLOWN FACE CAKE

1. Bake a round cake and frost with white icing.
2. Decorate top to make a silly clown face, using jellybeans, sprinkles, colored marshmallows, and licorice.
3. Let the kids make their own clown face cupcakes by providing a supply of icings, gels, sprinkles, and other edible decorations.

COSTUMES

- Ask the kids to come dressed as clowns, circus performers, ringmasters, animals, or acrobats.

DECORATIONS

- Stick a pole in the middle of the yard and drape a sheet over the top. Pull the ends out and attach them to trees or fences to make a big top circus tent.

- Fill the area with balloons, or tie the balloons together to make a big top tent.
- Make a three-ring circus by placing lengths of rope in circles on the ground. Make sure the circles are large enough for kids to perform inside.

GAMES

- Lion Taming: Have the players form a circle, facing in toward the middle—they are the lions. Choose one kid to be the ringmaster and have him or her walk around the outside of the lions' circle. The ringmaster must tag a lion, then run around the ring and make it back to where the lion was standing before the lion touches him or her. If the ringmaster makes it back, he or she is a lion. If not, he or she is "eaten" and is out of the game. Play until only one kid remains.
- Walk the Tightrope: Make a balance beam using an eight-to-ten foot long two-by-four placed on the ground. Have the tightrope walkers line up at one end. Give the kids increasingly difficult tasks to perform as they move across the balance beam, such as walking across normally, then sideways, then backwards, then with one arm in the air, then toe-to-heel, then with their eyes closed! Anyone who steps off the balance beam is out. Play until only one kid remains.

- Instead of using a sheet, create the feeling of a big top with crepe paper streamers by hanging them from the center of the party area to the outside. Twist the streamers and use different colors for a festive look.
- Get large appliance boxes and paint them to resemble animal cages. Cut out long slits along one side to make bars for the cage. Place large stuffed animals inside.

ACTIVITIES

- Juggling Act: Check with friends or the phone book to find someone to teach the kids how to juggle. Provide each kid with three balls, beanbags, or other items to juggle. When the kids get good at it, give them three different items to juggle, such as an apple, a sponge, and a ball. Make the juggling more and more challenging as they improve.
- Awesome Acrobats: Borrow some mats from a local gym or make your own from old mattress pads, air mattresses, or foam blocks. Let the kids do acrobatic stunts, such as tumbling and cartwheels in a follow-the-leader pattern.
- Clown Face: Purchase some colorful makeup from a party or toy store so the kids can paint their faces to look like clowns. Have mirrors handy, along with moistened towelettes and paper towels. Don't forget the Polaroid camera for instant take-home pictures.
- Stupid Pet Tricks: Have the kids act like animals and perform tricks. For example, you might tell one guest to be a kangaroo and have him or her hop

across the room backwards. Another might be an elephant and have to pick up a peanut with his or her toes.

FOOD

- Give the kids circus treats, such as bags of cotton candy, peanuts, popcorn, and so on.
- Make the kids hot dogs and offer a relish bar with a selection of trimmings.

FAVORS

- Give the guests tiny circus animals to take home for their own circus fun.
- Let the kids have a supply of face paints so they can make their own clown faces.
- Purchase small clown dolls and give one to each guest.
- Send the kids home with a popcorn ball, a bag of peanuts, or a caramel apple.

VARIATIONS

- Take the kids to a real circus.

HELPFUL HINTS

- Don't overdo the sugar. Be sure to give the kids a balanced meal before they eat too many of the goodies.

COOL IN THE POOL

For a hot time in the summer sun, host a Cool in the Pool party. All you need to do is lather on the sun block—the water will entertain the kids for hours. Just keep the towels handy for the soaking finale!

INVITATIONS

- Send the swimmers postcards of hotel swimming pools, beaches, or other water resorts, with party details on the back.
- Buy some inexpensive sunglasses and decorate them with puffy pens. Attach cards with party details. Mail to guests in small boxes.
- Pour a little water into small plastic containers, tint blue, and seal the lids shut with Super Glue. Write the party details on the containers with a felt-tip pen. Mail to guests in small boxes.

COSTUMES

- Have the kids wear their bathing suits. Ask them to also bring towels, coverups, and a change of clothes.

DECORATIONS

- Drape fishnets along the fence and attach plastic fish as if they have been caught.
- Set water toys around the party area, and place a rubber ducky on the table as a centerpiece.
- Fill the pool with inner tubes, beach balls, and other floating toys.

- Hang posters of tropical vacations on the fence or along the side of the house.
- Play Hawaiian or Beach Boys music in the background.

GAMES

- Super Marco Polo: To play the traditional version of Marco Polo, swimmers move around the pool while the player chosen as Marco Polo tries to find them with his or her eyes closed. When he or she calls out "Marco," the other swimmers must respond with "Polo." With Super Marco Polo, no one says anything and ALL the

swimmers must close their eyes! When Marco Polo catches a swimmer, the swimmer switches places with Marco.

- Escape from Jaws: One swimmer is chosen to play the shark and the rest of the swimmers must try to keep from being eaten by "Jaws" as they swim around the pool. Whoever the shark touches is out; play until only one swimmer remains.
- Frogman Jump or Dive: Swimmers line up behind the diving board. As the first player jumps off the end of the board, the next player in line calls out "Jump!" or "Dive!" The player must try to follow the command midair or he or she is out.
- Gold Diggers: Paint small rocks with gold paint. When dry, drop them onto the bottom of the pool. Have the swimmers stand around the pool. On the word "Go!" they all jump into the pool and try to retrieve as many gold nuggets as they can. The one with the most nuggets wins a prize.

POOL PARTY CAKE

1. Bake a sheet cake and frost with white frosting.
2. Tint some of the white frosting blue. Frost the center of the cake to make the pool.
3. Tint shredded coconut green with food coloring and sprinkle around the outside of the pool to make grass.
4. Insert plastic sharks in the pool for decoration.

- Pop the Piranha: Blow up balloons and toss them into the pool. Line the swimmers up around the pool. On the word "Go!" they must jump into the pool and try to pop as many balloons as they can. Whoever pops the most balloons wins.
- Rescue Rope: Toss some items that float into the pool, such as a chunk of wood, an inflated toy, and so on. Give one player a length of rope and have him or her try to lasso an item and bring it safely to shore. For a competition, give all the players a rope and have them race to bring their items to shore.
- Water Basketball: Buy a water basketball hoop or make your own using a small ring of plastic—a little larger than

beach ball. Have the first player in line jump into the pool while you throw the ball. The player must try to catch the ball and hold onto it as he or she lands in the water. If you have a diving board, have the players jump from it while trying to catch the ball.
- Give the kids watercolors and paper and let them paint a beach scene.

FOOD
- Serve the swimmers fish and chips to keep their energy levels up.
- Wash it down with Gatorade.
- Hand out Gummy Fish for a between-meal treat.

FAVORS
- Send the guests home with an inflatable pool toy, such as an inner tube or air mattress.
- Give the kids sunglasses to take home.
- Buy inexpensive beach towels and give one to each sunbather.
- Offer lunch baggies filled with Gummy Fish.

VARIATIONS
- Take the kids to the beach or a local community pool for the party.

HELPFUL HINTS
- Be sure all the kids can swim. Never leave the pool area unattended.

the ball—that will float in the pool. Divide the players into two teams and have them play basketball in the water. Another option is to play volleyball by stringing a net or rope across the pool.

ACTIVITIES
- Ocean in a Bottle: Give each guest an empty clear plastic water bottle. Have them fill the bottle three-quarters full with water, add several drops of food color, some glitter, and fill it the rest of the way with cooking oil. Seal the lid shut with Super Glue and let the kids enjoy their Ocean in a Bottle.
- Butterfinger Ball: Line up the players along the side of the pool. Stand on the other side of the pool with an inflatable

CRAZY CAMP-OUT

Hosting an overnighter in your own backyard is a great way to entertain the kids. The Crazy Camp-Out party provides lots of ideas for nighttime fun in your very own make-believe wilderness.

INVITATIONS

- Cut out tent-shaped cards from brown construction paper, with the fold at the top of the tent. Open the front of the tent and write the party details inside. Add a drawing of a kid in a sleeping bag.
- Send the campers a pack of freeze-dried food with the party details written on the back. Mail in small boxes or padded envelopes.
- Send postcards of famous national parks, such as Yellowstone or Yosemite, and write the party details on the back.

CAKE LOG

1. Bake a cake on a cookie sheet pan that has at least a half-inch edge. Because the cake is very thin, keep an eye on it so it doesn't burn.
2. Allow the cake to cool, then frost it with chocolate icing.
3. Sprinkle on chopped nuts, raisins, and seeds.
4. Beginning at one end, roll the cake lengthwise into a log.
5. Frost with more chocolate frosting, sprinkle with seeds and nuts, and cut into slices.

COSTUMES

- Ask the campers to come dressed in appropriate camping attire, with hiking boots, hats, and a jacket for the cold night air.
- Have the kids bring pajamas, sleeping bags, and other camping equipment to use at the party.
- Ask the guests to bring along any box games or comic books they might wish to share.

around the camping area. When night falls, the eyes will glow in the dark.
- Make owls out of construction paper and prop them on the fence.
- Set out camping equipment on a picnic table. Set the table with bandana place mats, personalized for each camper with puffy paints. Set a mini flashlight at each place.
- Once night falls, play tapes of nature sounds on a portable cassette player.

GAMES

- Flashlight Tag: When it gets dark, give one player a flashlight and have that player close his or her eyes and count to twenty while the other players hide. He or she then tries to spot the other players by shining the flashlight around the yard. Anyone who gets tagged by the light is out of the game. Play until everyone is caught, then select a new player to hold the flashlight.
- Name that Noise: Campers always seem to hear funny noises when they're out in the wilderness. For this game, tape-record a bunch of noises, such as a dog barking, a chain rattling, a door creak-

DECORATIONS

- Set up a large tent for the campers to sleep in. Borrow a few tents if you need to and make a tent village.
- Clear a space for a hibachi and make that your campfire. Set logs around the outside for the kids to sit on.
- Paint tagboard with glow-in-the-dark paint, then cut out dozens of eyes. Fill in the centers of the eyes with black felt-tip pen, then stick pairs of eyes all

ing, a motor running, a person screaming, and so on. After dark, gather the campers around the fire and play the tape-recorded noises. Stop the tape after each noise and let the kids write down what they think the noise is. Whoever gets the most noises correct wins a prize.

ACTIVITIES

- The Ghost that Never Dies Story: When it gets dark, have the campers sit around the campfire. Begin a spooky story about a ghost. Stop at an exciting part in the story. Have the next player continue the story, also ending at an exciting part. Continue until everyone has had a chance to add to the story.
- Midnight Hike: When it gets dark, have everyone hold hands in a long line. Lead the group on a midnight hike around the dark yard. Put up obstacles for the hikers to climb over, around, under, or through.
- Pass the Body Parts: When it gets dark, have everyone sit in a circle around the campfire. While you make up a story

about a body that falls apart, pass around bags with various "body parts" inside—peeled grapes for eyeballs, cooked spaghetti for brains, a peeled tomato for a heart, and so on. Let the kids feel all the body parts. Reveal the true contents of the bags when the story is over.

FOOD

- Roast hot dogs over the hibachi, serve s'mores for dessert, and hand out freeze-dried camp food for snacks.
- Give the kids water bottles filled with sports drinks so they can quench their thirst all night long.

FAVORS

- Send the campers home in the morning with mini flashlights, freeze-dried food, a compass, and a fresh selection of comic books.

VARIATIONS

- Take the kids camping at a real campground.

HELPFUL HINTS

- Sleep outside with the kids to make sure they stay safe and feel secure.

DINOSAUR PARK

Go back to the land before time with a Dinosaur Park party. During your expedition, you'll search for fossils, meet some prehistoric creatures, and have a few exciting adventures along the way!

INVITATIONS
- Buy large plastic eggs at the hobby or toy store. Write the party details on small pieces of paper, wrinkle the paper, dip in tea, then allow to dry. This will give the paper an "antique" look. Place the paper and a small plastic dinosaur inside the eggs and mail to the guests in small boxes or padded envelopes.
- Send the kids a dinosaur coloring book. Write the party details on each of the pages so they have to keep turning pages to read the entire invitation.

COSTUMES
- Ask the explorers to come dressed for the expedition as adventurers (like Indiana Jones), scientists in white lab coats (one of the parent's old white shirts), or cave men and women.

DECORATIONS
- Hang up posters of dinosaurs around the yard.
- Set dinosaur toys and stuffed animals on the party table and around the area.
- Cut out jungle trees, giant rocks, and a volcano from large sheets of construction paper and place them on the fence and walls.
- Set up a small scale Dinosaur Park scene using sand, small rocks, toy trees, and toy dinosaurs. Use as a centerpiece for the party table.

GAMES
- Dino Dig: Buy a bunch of toy plastic dinosaurs and bury them in the sandbox or just hide them throughout the backyard. Let the kids go on a dinosaur dig to find as many as they can. Whoever finds the most dinosaurs wins a prize.

- Don't Wake the Dino: Choose one player to be the Dinosaur and have him or her lie down on a towel on the ground. Set plastic eggs with a prize inside all around the Dinosaur. Have the Dinosaur close his or her eyes and pretend to be asleep. One at a time, the players must approach the sleeping Dinosaur and try to steal one of the prize eggs. If the Dinosaur opens his or her eyes and grabs the player, the player becomes the next sleeping Dinosaur and the Dinosaur gets the player's prize.
- Hot Lava: Create an obstacle path around the yard, using items the kids can step on or climb on, such as a large rock, a small chair, a large shoe, a

VOLCANO CAKE

1. Bake cake in a well-greased oven-proof bowl. Bake the cake a little longer than called for in the directions, until it is done in the middle.
2. Remove cake from bowl and turn over onto a large round plate.
3. Frost cake with chocolate icing, leaving the top bare.
4. Frost the top with red frosting, using tubes of icing.
5. Stick thin red licorice whips into the top of cake, shooting out like hot erupting lava.
6. Tint shredded coconut green with food coloring and sprinkle around plate. Add plastic toy dinosaurs.

piece of paper, a short ladder, and so on. Set the items close to each other but still challenging to reach. Have the kids cross the yard by stepping only on the items. Anyone who touches the "hot lava"—or ground—is out.

- Lost in the Jungle: Blindfold one player and walk him or her to a distant part of the yard. Spin the player around, and tell the player to find his or her way back to the rest of the kids. Repeat with all the players, starting them from different parts of the yard. Award prizes to the kids who return to "civilization" the fastest.

• Let the kids make their own dinosaur skeletons using kits from science or toy stores. Another option is to have the kids design their own dinosaur using Popsicle sticks.

FOOD

• Give the kids expedition foods, such as beef jerky, fruits and nuts in lunch baggies, and rock or crystal candy.
• Make the kids Dino Burgers with all the trimmings. Call the ketchup "hot lava," the mustard "jungle paste," and the relish "algae."

FAVORS

• Send the kids home with toy dinosaurs, dinosaur picture or coloring books, and dinosaur T-shirts.
• Give the kids a build-it-yourself dinosaur skeleton kit.
• Look around the toy store for anything related to dinosaurs—you're bound to find plenty of fun things to give the kids.

ACTIVITIES

• Grow-A-Saurus: Show the kids how to grow their own Dinosaur Plant! Give each guest a knee-high nylon stocking. At the bottom of the stocking, have them pour in a scoopful of lawn seeds. Then fill the stocking with potting soil until the nylon is nearly full, leaving room to tie off the top in a knot. Set the Dino, knot-side-down, into a small plastic bowl. Let the kids glue on wiggly eyes and add a felt cutout mouth, ears, and tail. Gently water the top of the Dino. Tell the kids to take home their Grow-A-Sauruses and in a few days their Dinosaur Plants will grow spikes!

VARIATIONS

• Take the kids to a museum that features dinosaur fossils.

HELPFUL HINTS

• Read a book or watch a video about dinosaurs at the beginning of the party to get the kids in the mood for the party.

DOWN ON THE FARM PARTY

Say goodbye to city life and gather the young farmers for a day in the barnyard. There's plenty to do down on the farm. So rise and shine, it's farming time!

INVITATIONS

- Cut out pictures of farms from farming magazines and mount them on construction paper. Write party details around the pictures and mail to guests.
- Fill small boxes with tiny plastic farm animals, write party details on packets of vegetable seeds, and mail to guests.
- Send the kids bandanas with the party details written in felt-tip pen around the outside edge.
- Write the party details on gourds and send them in boxes to the kids.

COSTUMES

- Ask the guests to come dressed as farmers in overalls or jeans and plaid

FARM CAKE

1. Bake a sheet cake, preferably a carrot cake.
2. Frost with chocolate frosting.
3. Tint shredded coconut green with food coloring and sprinkle over the cake.
4. Set toy farm animals on one part of the cake and a small farmhouse on another. Create a tiny vegetable garden using small candies.

shirts. Provide the accessories when they arrive—neckerchiefs, straw hats, and corncob pipes.
- Suggest they come dressed as a favorite farm animal for some silly fun.
- Have them wear square dance costumes to the party.

GAMES

- Animal Antics: For the first round of Animal Antics, sit the kids in a circle. Have each kid draw a card that has the name or picture of an animal on it. The kids take turns making the sound of the animal while the other players try to guess what it is. For the second round, reshuffle the cards and have the kids draw a new animal. Each kid then walks or moves like the animal while everyone guesses what it is.

- Don't Break the Eggs: Divide the players into two teams and line them up. Give all the players a spoon. Place an egg on the spoons of the first player for each team. Have the kids race back and forth across the yard, holding the egg in the spoon. When they return to their team's line, they must transfer the egg to the next player's spoon—without touching the egg with their hands—so the next player can continue the race. The first team to finish without breaking an egg wins.

- Horseshoe Hijinks: Set up a game of horseshoes and teach the kids how to play. Try some variations on the game, such as playing blindfolded, in teams, tossing under a leg, and so on.

- Taste Test: Seat the players around the picnic table. Place a variety of cut-up fruits and vegetables on the table, covered in foil so they aren't visible. Have the kids close their eyes, then pass around the cut-up foods and let them guess what they are tasting.

DECORATIONS

- Buy or make your own farm animal posters and hang them on the fence.
- Pile up straw to make a haystack. Use bales of hay for seating around a picnic table.
- Hang a cowbell to call the farmers in when it's mealtime.
- Play square dance music in the background.

ACTIVITIES

- Go to a farm and let the kids pick their own fruits and veggies. You could also hide a number of fruits and veggies around the backyard and have the kids hunt for them.
- Square Dance: Hire a square dance caller and teach the kids how to square dance! Have them dress up in costume to make it more fun.
- Petting Zoo: Ask a petting zoo or pet shop to bring an animal to the party so the kids can see it, pet it, and feed it. Consider getting a goat, a chicken or duck, a rabbit, or even a horse.

FOOD

- Make Pigs in a Blanket by wrapping biscuit dough around cocktail wieners and baking according to the biscuit directions.
- Prepare a variety of fruit or veggie dips and let the kids dip slices of apple, banana, pineapple, carrot, celery, and green pepper strips into the dips.
- Create a fancy egg omelet to each guest's individual order. Have lots of ingredients to choose from.
- Bake or fry some chicken legs and serve them with corn on the cob, baked beans, and biscuits for a classic farm dinner.
- Don't forget to ring the dinner bell when it's time to chow down.

VARIATIONS

- Take a tour of a local farm for an up close and personal look at farming life.
- Visit a petting zoo and let the kids enjoy the animals.

HELPFUL HINTS

- Make sure none of the guests are allergic to animals if you plan to have animals visit the party.

FAVORS

- Send the farmers home with small farm animals.
- Let the kids keep the accessories—the bandanas, the hats, and so on.
- Give each kid a book about farms.
- Make a basket of fruit and give one to each guest.

FRISBEE PARTY

A Frisbee Party? Why not! All you need is a big play area, a bright sunny day, and lots and lots of Frisbees. The kids can play games, have races, do stunts and tricks, all with their little plastic disks.

INVITATIONS

- Buy tiny plastic Frisbees from the toy store, write the party details on them with permanent felt-tip pen, and mail in padded envelopes to the guests.
- Cut out Frisbee-sized circles from yellow posterboard, draw a sun on the front, and write the party details on the back. Mail to guests in large envelopes.

COSTUMES

- Ask the kids to incorporate mini Frisbees with their outfits, such as make one a hat, attach another as a necklace, and so on.
- Have the kids wear athletic clothes so they are comfortable while playing.

DECORATIONS

- Buy a bunch of Frisbees in a variety of colors. Hang from the fence, place them on the table, and display them throughout the yard.
- Cut out paper Frisbees from colorful paper and hang them around the yard.

GAMES

- Frisbee Free-for-All: Gather the players in a circle and give each of them a Frisbee. At the word "Go!" have them toss their Frisbees across the circle to the opposite players, while trying to catch any Frisbee that comes their way! The game is chaos, so it should be challenging and fun.

- Frisbee Golf: Buy some inexpensive wicker baskets from the hobby store and attach a rope to each handle. Tie the baskets to various trees or other tall points so that the baskets hang about chest-high to the kids. Give all the kids Frisbees and place them several yards from the starting basket. Each kid gets two chances to toss their Frisbees into the basket; if a kid misses on the first throw, he or she throws again from wherever the Frisbee landed. Each player gets one point for each basket he or she makes. When all the players have had their two throws, the whole group moves to the next basket and tries again. Whoever gets the most points wins.
- Frisbee Hop: Line two teams up three yards apart and facing each other; each team's player should be a few feet apart from their fellow teammates. Give every player—except for the first kid on

each team—a flexible Frisbee. The players without Frisbees then stand at either end of the space between the teams. On the word "Go!" they must try to walk across the path while the players from the other team try to tag their feet with a low-flying Frisbee toss. Anyone who is tagged it out. Repeat with all the players. The team that lasts the longest wins.
- Frisbee Marathon: Divide the players into two-man teams; give one player on each team a Frisbee. Have them stand five or six yards apart, with plenty of

space around. On the word "Go!" have the players toss the Frisbee back and forth, in a competition. Any team that drops their Frisbee is out. The last team left wins a prize.

ACTIVITIES

• Frisbee Face: Give each guest a standard-sized Frisbee. Provide felt-tip pens, puffy paints, glitter, decals, and stickers, and let the kids decorate their Frisbees into funny faces. Award a prize for the silliest, ugliest, funniest, most beautiful, and most familiar looking.

• Frisbee Tower: Purchase a bunch of mini Frisbees and place them in a pile in the middle of the yard. Have the guests divide the Frisbees among themselves. The first player begins the activity by placing one of his or her Frisbees on the ground. Each of the following players places his or her Frisbee on top of the first Frisbee, and the action continues until someone causes the growing tower to topple!

FOOD

• Offer the kids Frisbee foods—round crackers with cheese, apples cut into round slices, and mini pizzas.
• Have lots of sports drinks handy for the thirsty Frisbee players.

FAVORS

• Send the kids sailing home with all sizes, colors, and designs of Frisbees.

VARIATIONS

• Take the kids to one of the many Frisbee Golf Courses popping up around the country, or make your own at a local park where you have plenty of room to toss the disks.

HELPFUL HINTS

• Be sure to have plenty of Frisbees on hand in case some go flying over the fence!

GARDEN PARTY

The backyard garden—whether real or created just for this event—is the foundation for a great outdoor party. There are lots of games and activities to turn all the guests' thumbs green, so dig in!

INVITATIONS

- Buy seed packets from the garden store and write the party details in permanent felt-tip pen on the backs. Enclose in envelopes and mail to the invited gardeners.
- Mail an apple to each guest in a small box. Write the party details on a card and tie it to the stem. Include a recipe for baked apples.
- Buy some artificial flowers and mail them to guests in decorative bunches. Attach a card with the party details.

COSTUMES

- Ask the kids to come dressed as gardeners or tell them to decorate their clothes with artificial or real leaves and flowers.

FLOWER CAKE

1. Bake a sheet or round cake according to package directions.
2. Frost with white icing.
3. Tint shredded coconut green with food coloring and sprinkle all over cake.
4. Top with edible flowers or candy flowers.

DECORATIONS

- Tie paper flowers around the yard.
- Hang large posters of vegetables and fruits, available at the teacher supply store.
- Set real or plastic fruits and vegetables on the table. Create a funny monster out of fruits and veggies for the centerpiece.

GAMES

- Funny Foods: Buy unusual looking foods at gourmet or ethnic food stores, such as turnips, kumquats, poi, celery root,

- Taste and Tell: Cut an onion in half and set it on the table. Gather the kids around the table, blindfold one of them, then give him or her a small piece of a vegetable or fruit to taste. Before tasting the item, the kid must take a whiff of the onion to help disguise the taste. Award prizes for correct answers and repeat with all the kids.

ACTIVITIES

- Garden Glove Puppet: Give a single garden glove to every guest. Provide a variety of items used in creating finger puppets, such as small pompoms, wiggly eyes, tiny hats, felt, puffy paints, felt-tip pens, and so on, then let the kids make their own Garden Glove Puppets.
- Name Garden: Give each guest a flat metal tray, such as a small cookie sheet or tin box. Fill the tray with a layer of potting soil. Have the kids "write" their names in the soil using grass seeds. Spray the dirt lightly with water and set in indirect sunlight for the rest of the party, then send them home with the gardeners. In a few days their names will begin to grow!
- Portable Greenhouse: Draw outlines of greenhouses on green construction paper. Cut out the center of each greenhouse, leaving a one-inch edge around the outside, then distribute the outlines with plastic lunch baggies to the kids.

and so on. Display the items one at a time and have the players guess what each one is. If they don't know, have them make up a funny name for the food item. Award food prizes for the most correct answers.

- Sweet as a Rose: Buy a variety of fragrant flowers at the florist and put them together in a vase. At game time, have the kids close their eyes. Pull out one flower, pass it around to the players in a circle, and have them identify the flower based on its smell. Award prizes for correct answers.

Have them moisten a paper towel, fold it in half, and place it in the bottom of the baggie. Rest five beans or seeds on top of the towel. Tape the cutout greenhouse around the baggie, as a frame, then tape the house to a window. Have the guests take their framed baggies home and place them on their own windows.

- Veggie Monster: Place a number of small vegetables and fruits on the table. Ask the kids to create a Veggie Monster, using toothpicks to attach the different pieces of fruits and veggies. Award prizes for the ugliest, the most creative, the prettiest, the funniest, the scariest, and so on.
- Sunflower Seeds: Buy a whole sunflower and let the kids pick off the seeds. Place seeds on a cookie sheet, baste with oil, sprinkle with salt, and roast in oven until lightly browned. Eat them when they're cool.

VARIATIONS
- Take the kids to a real community garden. Let them plant or pick real fruits and vegetables.

HELPFUL HINTS
- Check to see if the guests are allergic to any of the foods you will be serving or using for games.

FOOD
- Serve a variety of cut-up fruits and vegetables skewered together on sticks. Offer fruit and veggie dips on the side.
- Set out bowls of seeds and nuts for the kids to munch on during activities.
- Make Garden Face Sandwiches. First make peanut butter and jelly sandwiches, then decorate the top of each sandwich with fruits and vegetables cut up to resemble funny faces.

FAVORS
- Give the kids seed packets to take home.
- Offer the guests a gardening kit consisting of garden gloves, a trowel, a mist sprayer, seeds, and so on.
- Give the guests books on gardening for kids so they can grow things at home.

GLADIATOR GAMES

Hercules and Xena are here to help you make your Gladiator Games Party a glorious success. Test the strength and endurance of your guests as they play the parts of mighty men and wonder women.

INVITATIONS

- Buy postcard-sized pictures of the kids' favorite American Gladiators from television, photos of Hercules and Xena, superheroes, or pictures of famous wrestling stars. Write your party details on the backs of the pictures and mail to guests.
- Buy Power Bars for the guests, attach a card with the party details, and invite them to the Gladiator Games.
- Prepare fill-in-the-blank scorecards for the games and mail with the party details. Beside each guest's name, write "Winner!"

COSTUMES

- Ask the kids to come dressed as their favorite superheroes, gladiators, or as Hercules and Xena.
- If you prefer, have the kids dress in sport clothing or sweats so they can play the games easily and not worry about their costumes.

DECORATIONS

- Buy posters of the Gladiators, Hercules and Xena, and favorite superheroes and post them on the fence and side of the house.
- Set up trophies on the table. Mark each place setting with a red ribbon.
- Write out scorecards on large sheets of poster board, listing the names of the games and the contestants. Post the cards so everyone can see them.
- Dress up the yard with colorful streamers and balloons to make a festive arena for play.

GAMES

- Blind Walk: Test the kids' bravery with a Blind Walk. Create an obstacle path from one end of the yard to the other. Line up the contestants and let them have a good look at the path. One at a time, blindfold the gladiators and have them walk the path without looking. Note each player's time on the scorecard.
- Gold Coin Toss: Test the kids' arm strength and depth perception. Buy a bunch of chocolate gold coins. Set a small bucket in the middle of the yard and have the gladiators line up about ten feet from it. One at a time, let each player try to toss ten gold coins into the bucket. Award one point for each coin that goes in. Let each player keep the coins that make it into the container.
- Hacky Sack: Test the kids' flexibility and coordination. Divide the group into pairs; give each pair a hacky sack. On the word "Go!" have the pairs pass the hacky sack back and forth using their

feet. Award points to the pair that lasts the longest without letting their hacky sack touch the ground. Repeat several times.

- Rope Cross: Test the kids' arm strength and stamina. Tie a rope from one end of a tree to another sturdy object. Have each gladiator travel along the rope without touching the ground. Time the players as they cross the rope; give points for the best times.
- Tug of War: Test the group's strength. Divide the players into two teams. Have the teams stand in a line opposite each other, about five feet apart. Place a long rope in the center, giving the ends to each team. On the word "Go!" have the teams try to pull one another across a

GLADIATOR ARENA CAKE

1. Make a sheet cake and frost with green icing.
2. Set tiny figurines on top, such as Hercules and Xena, Gladiators, superheroes, or wrestlers.
3. Give action and stunt poses to the figures on the cake.
4. Add gold coins around the outside for a sparkling decoration.

- Mystery Masks: Cut masks out of stiff posterboard. Let the kids decorate the masks using fabric pieces, sequins and glitter, felt-tip pens, feathers, and glue. Have the guests give themselves mysterious names to match their masks.

FOOD
- Make a long Hero Sandwich by filling a loaf of French bread with meats, cheeses, lettuce, and tomato. Slice off sections as needed.
- Provide power drinks with the sandwiches to give the kids energy to continue the games.
- Offer gold coin candies as a dessert treat.

FAVORS
- Give the kids medallions, ribbons, trophies, medals, and other awards based on the number of points they earned playing the games.
- Offer posters of the kids' heroes to take home. Give them the figures from the cake.

middle line. Award points to all the players on the winning team.
- Rope Walk: Test the kids' balance. Lay a thick rope out on the yard, curving it around in a maze-like fashion. Have the gladiators walk along the rope. Mark points off each time they lose their balance and step off the rope.

ACTIVITIES
- Gladiator Garb: Make Gladiator accessories for the kids' costumes by having them create their own wrist and ankle bands. Let them cut out strips of colored felt, wrap the strips around their wrists and ankles, and use self-sticking Velcro to secure them. Make sweatbands the same way.

VARIATIONS
- Take the kids to a wrestling match or a movie about Hercules and Xena.

HELPFUL HINTS
- Make sure the losers also receive fun prizes.

GOPHER GOLF

Gopher Golf offers a twist on the conventional nine-hole golf game adults play—it's more creative, more challenging, and lots more fun. Grab your caddy; it's time to tee off!

INVITATIONS

- Buy second-hand golf balls from the golf store or a local golf course and write the party details on the balls, using permanent felt-tip pens. Hand deliver or place in small boxes or padded envelopes and mail.
- On construction paper, draw out a golf course. At each hole, draw a triangular flag and write the party details in the flag. Color the course green and mail to the guests.

COSTUMES

- Ask the golfers to wear imitations of traditional golf leisurewear—slacks, collared T-shirt, and tennis shoes.

HOLE-IN-ONE CAKE

1. Make a sheet cake and frost with green icing.
2. Tint shredded coconut green with food coloring and sprinkle on the cake.
3. Outline golf course with chocolate frosting tube.
4. Stick small paper flags at the holes.
5. Use mini marshmallows for golf balls.

- Have the kids come dressed in athletic wear, sweats, shorts, and T-shirts.
- Buy inexpensive golf-themed T-shirts and distribute to the players as they arrive.

DECORATIONS

- Set up the backyard to look like a golf course. Encircle grassy areas with rope to make the individual greens and use a gardener's bulb planter to make the holes. Stick flags in the ground at each

GAMES

- Blindman's Golf: Once you've set up a miniature golf course in the yard, have players divide into two- or foursomes and play—without looking. Each time they are about to strike the ball, they must close their eyes! For added fun, award prizes for the best scores.
- Frisbee Golf: Instead of holes set in the ground, make the holes hang in the air! Attach red construction paper circles— each about the size of a Frisbee—to trees and fences around the yard. Have the kids walk through the course, one at a time, and try to hit each target. If any-one misses, they must pick up their Frisbee, wait their turn, and try again from the spot where the Frisbee landed. If they hit the mark, they are free to move on to the next target.
- Golf Challenge: Divide the group into two teams, then divide the yard in half. Have each team design a golf course for the other team. Tell the teams to be as cre-ative as possible. When both teams have finished nine holes, each team plays the other team's course. Award a prize to the team that designs the best course.
- Goofy Golf: In this game of miniature golf, the kids must be creative with the clubs, balls, and holes. For example, at the first hole have the golfers use broomsticks to hit oranges onto plates. At the second hole, let the kids use baseball bats to hit walnuts into tipped-

hole. If you don't want to make holes in your yard, another option is to use tipped-over tin cans.

- Along the fence, hang posters of golfing greats, such as Tiger Woods and Arnold Palmer. For fun, hang movie posters of funny golfers, such as Adam Sandler or Bill Murray.
- Write the guests' names on golf tees and set on the table to mark places. Set out clubs and golf balls for a center-piece.

over shoes. Use your imagination and think up other ways to play Goofy Golf.

- Peewee Golf: Set up a Peewee Golf course on the picnic table for a new challenge. Cover the table with a white sheet, and draw a course using green felt-tip pens. Use small cans or boxes tipped on their sides as holes. Give the players pencils and have them hit marbles along the course and into the holes.
- Team Golf: Play a game of miniature golf with the kids divided into teams. Have the first players on each team hit the ball, then the second player, then the third, and so on until each team sinks their shot. Play until all the teams complete the golf course.

ACTIVITIES

- Golf Ball Babies: Give each guest a golf ball to decorate with permanent felt-tip pens. Encourage them to personalize their golf balls by drawing funny little golf faces.
- Let the kids decorate the Frisbees, too.

VARIATIONS

- Take the golfers out to the greens and let them play nine holes of real golf or eighteen holes of miniature golf.

HELPFUL HINTS

- Have the kids stand back when golf clubs are swinging so no one gets hurt.

- Let the kids make their own golfing T-shirts using felt-tip pens, puffy paints, and decals.

FOOD

- In keeping with the theme of miniature golf, make a variety of miniature foods. Serve tiny sandwiches, mini crackers and cheese, and small shots of soda.
- Set the table like a golf course. Place the snacks and treats at the different holes, include greens for the green, cherry tomatoes for the golf balls, and celery sticks for the golf clubs.

FAVORS

- Send the golfers home with a set of colored golf balls and a handful of tees spray-painted gold.
- Get the kids a cartoon or humorous golf book.
- Give the guests discount coupons to use at local miniature or full-sized golf courses.

HAYRIDE PARTY

Hey! Who wants to go to a Hayride Party? There's nothing like a hayride to provide an afternoon or evening of fun, songs, and games. So hitch up the wagon—it's time for some horsing around!

INVITATIONS

- Draw hay wagons on the lower halves of sheets of construction paper. Fold the top halves of the paper over to make covered wagons, glue in some hay, and write the party details inside. Mail to guests.
- Tie up small bundles of hay and stick them inside envelopes. Attach party details and mail to guests.
- Cut out pictures of horses and glue them onto construction paper. Write party details on the back and mail to the guests.
- Write party details on inexpensive bandannas and mail to the guests.

COSTUMES

- Ask the guests to wear overalls, jeans, or square dance skirts; flannel or plaid shirts; and bandannas as accessories.
- Suggest the kids wear their hair in pigtails or sticking out like Tom Sawyer. Offer to pencil in freckles with a lip line or makeup pencil when the kids arrive.
- Give the kids farmer hats when they arrive.

DECORATIONS

- Enhance the starting point of your party with bales of hay or a haystack.
- Make a scarecrow to greet the guests by stuffing old clothes with hay. An easy way to prop up the scarecrow is to sit it in a chair.

GAMES

- Hay! Watch Out! While you're waiting for the hayride to start, play this game of skill and balance. Set up some hay bales

a couple of feet apart and have the kids try to step from one bundle to the next without falling off. Make it easy to begin with and harder near the end by moving the bundles farther and farther apart.

- Who's Missing? Have the kids close their eyes. Tap one person to be it and cover him or her in a pile of hay. Tell the rest of the guests to open their eyes and guess who's missing. The first one to yell out the missing player's name gets a point. Repeat with other kids.

ACTIVITIES

- Hay Ride: Use the phone book to locate someone who hosts hayrides. Nearly every community has a rural area with a farm that offers this fun activity. Then book your date and hire the hayride for an afternoon or evening.
- Harmonica Hayfest: Provide harmonicas to all the guests so they can play some tunes on the hayride. Teach the kids how to play a few simple tunes, such as

HAYRIDE CAKE

1. Bake a sheet cake and frost with chocolate icing.
2. Tint coconut yellow with food coloring and sprinkle over the top of cake to make hay.
3. Set a small covered wagon and a couple of plastic horses on top to make a hayride wagon.

"She'll be Coming 'Round the Mountain," "On Top of Old Smokey (or Spaghetti)," or "Over the River and Through the Woods."

- Hayride Songfest: When the kids get tired of the harmonicas, let them sing songs as they ride around the farm or ranch. Bring along an inexpensive songbook for ideas and lyrics. You can also make photocopies of the words if you prefer the kids to sing on their own. Great songs for hayrides include: "Old MacDonald," "Row, Row, Row Your Boat," and "Make New Friends."
- Hay Painting: Cover the picnic table with newspapers. Give each guest several

sheets of white paper. Set out poster paints and sprinkle the table with hay. Have the kids paint their pictures on the paper using the hay as brushes.

- Scarecrow: Gather some old clothes, accessories, such as eyeglasses, hats, gloves, scarves, and jewelry, and lots of hay. Divide the group into teams and have each team create their own scarecrow.

FOOD

- Have a picnic on your hayride with easy-to-eat sandwiches, chips, and canned drinks.

- Make Chocolate Haystacks for dessert. Melt chocolate chips in a small pot, pour in shredded wheat cereal, and cover with chocolate. Heap spoonfuls of the concoction onto waxed paper. Serve when cool.
- Give the kids trail mix for the hayride trail.

FAVORS

- Send the kids home with plastic farm animals or small plastic horses.
- Give the guests bandannas to wear home.
- Let the kids keep their harmonicas.
- Give the kids farmer hats to wear home.
- Buy inexpensive books about horses and pass them out to the kids.

VARIATIONS

- Instead of a hayride, find a local stable and let the kids go horseback riding.

HELPFUL HINTS

- Be sure none of the kids is allergic to hay or animals before they go on the ride.

HIDE 'N' HUNT

All kids love treasure hunts—the suspense of the search, the joy of discovery! There are so many variations on this Hide 'N' Hunt party that you can easily come up with your own exciting versions!

INVITATIONS

- Make Treasure Chest invitations by cutting out rectangles from brown construction paper. Fold each rectangle in half to make a treasure chest. Use a felt-tip pen to draw a chest on the outside of the cards. Write the party details inside, then glue on sequins or jewels.
- Send the guests on a treasure hunt for their invitations! Hide five clues around each guest's front yard, then mail the first clue to begin the hunt. Let the last clue lead the guest to the party invitation.
- Write out the party details on a large sheet of construction paper. Cut or tear the paper into pieces, taking care to keep the individual words intact. Send one or two words to each guest with a

note that the other guests have the rest of the pieces. (Be sure to provide their names and phone numbers.) The guests will have to call each other to get all the words to the invitation, then unscramble them to figure out the party details.

COSTUMES

- Ask the guests to wear pirate outfits—eye patches, bandannas, striped shirts, and pirate hats.

TREASURE CHEST CAKE

1. Bake a sheet cake and frost with chocolate icing.
2. Frost the cake pan and set it at a right angle to the cake to look like the open lid of a treasure chest.
3. Decorate with frosting tubes.
4. Place chocolate gold coins and candy jewelry on the cake.

• Have the kids dress as archeologists searching for buried treasures of the past.

• Have a mystery hunt and ask the guests to come as a favorite detective.

DECORATIONS

• Find some cardboard gift boxes, spray-paint them gold, and set them around the party area as treasure chests. Fill them with chocolate gold coins or inexpensive jewelry from thrift stores.

• Cover the table with white paper. Draw a treasure map on it using colorful felt-tip pens. Have the map lead the guests to their favors or the party cake. Provide different clues to the goodies at each place setting.

GAMES

• Buried Treasure Hunt: Hide a number of plastic toys and jewelry in the backyard. Divide the group into teams and give each team a list of poetic clues, such as "Roses are red, Violets are blue, My garden grows gems, Can you find one or two?" The team that finds the most items wins. Let the kids keep what they find.

• Following Footsteps: Draw out clues to a special treasure on the back of cutout footprints. Set the first footprint at the starting line and have the kids read the clue and try to figure out where the next clue is hidden. For added fun, hide two different sets of clues and have the kids search for the treasure as competing teams.

• Litter Pickup: Take the kids to the park and divide them into teams. Give each team a paper bag and have them race to collect as much litter as they can find in the park. Have the teams return at a designated time. Award a prize to the team who finds the most trash.

• Treasure Hunt: Divide the kids into two teams; put one team in the front yard and the other team in the backyard. Give each team paper and pencil. Have them bury a prize somewhere, then create a map that will lead to the treasure. The teams then switch maps and get to search for the other team's buried treasure.

- Treasure Surprise Ball: Buy enough different small toys so each guest will get one. Get a long crepe-paper streamer; wrap the first toy with the streamer until it is shaped like a small ball. Place another toy on the crepe-paper ball and continue to wrap until that toy is also covered. Keep adding toys and wrapping them until all the toys have been included. Tape the end closed. Seat the guests in a circle and play some music while the players pass the ball to each other. When the music stops, the player holding the ball gets to unwrap it slowly until he or she finds a toy. That player is then out of the game. Play until everyone has a toy.

them paint the boxes gold, then decorate the boxes with puffy paints, felt-tip pens, jewels, sequins, glitter, play coins, and other shiny items. The kids can then take the chests home and fill them with their own treasures.

ACTIVITIES

- Treasure Chests: Have the kids make their own treasure chests. Ask each kid to bring a shoebox to the party. Let

FOOD

- Make sandwiches and cut them into puzzle pieces. Place the pieces on a plate and let the kids try to match them before they eat.
- Give the kids candy coins, rings, and necklaces to eat.

VARIATIONS

- Host the party at a local archeological park so the kids can see some true buried treasure.

HELPFUL HINTS

- Make sure there is enough treasure for everyone so no one feels slighted.

FAVORS

- Send the kids home with surprise balls and candy coins.
- Give them books about buried treasures, pirate adventures, archeology discoveries, or famous mysteries.

HOLLYWOOD STUNTS

Spend a day in Hollywood for some behind-the-scenes action and fun. Show the kids how those miraculous movie stunts and tricks happen. Lights, camera, action!

INVITATIONS

- Buy postcards of famous action stars from Hollywood, such as Jackie Chan, Xena, Hercules, and so on, or buy postcards of stunt scenes from movies. Write the party details on the backs and mail to guests.

- Make your own invitations that will surprise and amaze your guests. Cut rectangles from stiff white paper and fold in half to make cards. On separate sheets of paper, cut out stars that are a little smaller than the size of the folded cards. Write "Hollywood Stunt Party" in the center of the stars; write the party details around the inside edges of the folded cards. Color the stars and add glitter. Cut out small rectangles of paper and fold the two ends in a zigzag. Glue the stars to the tops of the strips, then glue down the ends of the strips to the inside centers of the cards. Fold the cards, carefully pressing down the stars. When the cards are opened, the stars will jump out at the readers.

COSTUMES

- Ask the kids to come dressed in shorts and T-shirts, athletic sweat suits, or other flexible clothes.

- Have the kids come dressed as a favorite action movie star.

DECORATIONS

- Decorate the party area with cutout stars featuring action words such as "Pow," "Blam," "Bonk," and so on. Use a few of the stars as personalized place mats by writing the kids' names on them.
- Hang posters of famous movie action scenes.
- Play music from action movies such as *Indiana Jones* or *Hercules*.

GAMES

- Bicycle Slalom: Have the kids bring their bikes. Set up an obstacle course and have them slalom their bikes through the course. Award prizes to the kids who complete the course in the fastest times.
- Binocular Walk: Have the kids walk an obstacle course while looking through the wrong end of a pair of binoculars. Award prizes for the kids who complete the course in the best time.
- Cliffhanger: Let the kids walk on a tightrope—a thick rope placed on the round—without looking. Anyone who touches the ground is out. Repeat with harder and harder tricks, such as walking backwards, sideways, and so on, until only one kid remains.
- Do-It Dice: Make a giant pair of dice by taping together six equal-sized squares of cardboard per die. Write a stunt on each side of the dice, such as "Hop on one foot," "Walk backwards," and so on. Have the players take turns rolling the

dice and then acting out the required stunts. For example, if one die rolls up "Hop on one foot," and the other rolls up "Sing the alphabet backwards," the player must do both stunts at once.

- Falling Statues: Have two players stand on flat squares of cardboard placed three feet apart. Give each kid opposite ends of a rope and have them try to pull each other off their cardboard squares. Whoever falls off first loses the bout. Repeat with all the kids until one kid is crowned as the grand champion.
- Hula Hoopers: Give the kids Hula Hoops and have them perform designated tricks, such as "Hula Hoop in slow motion," "Hula Hoop super fast," "Use your neck," "Try your arms," and so on.

STUNT CAKE

1. Bake a sheet cake and frost with a favorite icing.
2. Decorate the cake with stars using tubes of frosting and sprinkles of confetti candy.
3. Cut pieces for all the kids and place on plates.
4. The kids must eat their cake without using their hands or silverware.

- Leapin' Limbo: Have the kids jump over a stick as it rises higher and higher, then have them limbo under the stick as it gets lower and lower. Anyone who touches the stick is out.
- Target Ball: Choose one player to stand against a wall; line the other players up several feet opposite him or her. Give the first kid in the line a ball and have him or her try to hit the player at the wall while the player does stunts called out by the other kids, such as "Jump," "Spin around," "Run back and forth," and so on. The player gets to do stunts until he or she is tagged, at which time the player gets in line and the kid who tagged the player goes to the wall.

ACTIVITIES

- Divide the kids into two teams and let them design a stunt for the other team. Have the first team show how to do the stunt, then have the second team do it—if they can.
- Let the kids make their own stunt shirts using inexpensive white T-shirts, felt-tip pens, puffy paints, stickers, and other decorations.

FOOD

- Give the kids a high-protein meal to keep up their strength during the stunts, such as a do-it-yourself hamburger or taco bar.
- Supply sports drinks for the thirsty players.

FAVORS

- Send the kids home with stunt books and collecting cards from action movies.

VARIATIONS

- Take the kids to a stunt show or an action movie, or rent a video full of action and stunt scenes.

HELPFUL HINTS

- Make sure you watch the kids carefully as they perform their stunts so they don't get carried away and do anything dangerous.

KITE-FLYING PARTY

The next time someone tells you to "Go fly a kite," throw a Kite-Flying Party! Your guests will love making and flying their own one-of-a-kind kites. Up, up, and away!

INVITATIONS

- Cut out tiny kites from construction paper, attach string with tiny bows for tails, and detail the kites with felt-tip pens. Write the party details on the backs and mail to guests.
- Cut off lengths of string about three feet long and six small pieces of fabric into rectangles the size of dollar bills. Write a few words of the party details on each piece of fabric. Tie the fabric to the strings, wind them up, and stuff into envelopes. The guests must pull out the

strings and untie the fabric from the kite tails to read the party instructions.
- Copy a photo of a child flying a kite and write the party details on the back. Mail to guests.
- Using origami books as instruction guides, fold the paper into kite shapes. Write the party details on the kites and mail to guests.

KITE CAKE

1. Bake a sheet cake. Cut off the corners to make a diamond shape.
2. Frost the cake with white icing and make fun kite designs with tubes of colored icing.
3. Attach a length of licorice rope to make the tail.
4. If you prefer, cover the cake with shredded coconut tinted green with food coloring to simulate grass. Attach tiny paper diamonds to stiff gardening or craft wire. Stick them into the cake and you have kites flying over a grassy field.

COSTUMES

- Ask the kids to come dressed as pilots, aviators, astronauts, parachuters, flight attendants, and so on.

• Have the kids make feather hats and wear them at the party so they can pretend to be birds.

DECORATIONS

• Buy inexpensive, colorful paper kites and set them along the fence or the walls of the house.
• Make some interesting kite tails using a variety of lightweight, printed fabrics.
• Draw a giant kite on a white paper tablecloth and let the kids color it when they arrive.

• Hang kites overhead to make a kite canopy.
• Make tiny kites for place settings. Personalize them with the guests' names.

GAMES

• Kite-Flying Adventure: Space the kids apart and let them raise their kites one at a time into the air. Or have a race and see who can get their kite flying first.
• Kite Puzzle: Buy two paper kites and cut them into large-sized puzzle pieces. Mix up the pieces to each kite, then divide the kids into two teams and see which team can be the first to put their puzzle kite back together!
• Kite Relay: Divide the group into two teams and line them up. Give the first player on each team a kite. On the word "Go!" the kite-holding players must race across the yard and back—with the kite flying a few feet in the air—then pass it off to the next player in line on his or her team. The first team to finish racing everyone wins a prize.

- Kite Race: Give everyone equal amounts of string, then see who can raise their kites the highest in one minute. Determine the height by measuring the amount of string let out from the roll.

ACTIVITIES

- Kite-Making Fun: Get some books on kite-making from the library or bookstore. Provide the kids with the proper materials and some art supplies, then let them create their own unique kites. Or simply buy plain kites at the store and let the kids decorate them with puffy paints and felt-tip pens.
- Kite Tails: Have the kids make up their own interesting kite tails out of different kinds of paper and fabric. Then have them bet on which ones will help the kite fly and which ones won't. Run test flights to see who guessed correctly.
- Kite Origami: Get origami books from the library or bookstore and teach the kids how to make tiny kites out of colored paper.

VARIATIONS

- Take the kids to a park so they'll have plenty of room to fly their kites.

HELPFUL HINTS

- Practice making and flying the kites first so you can teach the kids how to make their own kites and how to get them up in the air.

FOOD

- Make Kite Sandwiches out of bread and cheese cut them into diamond shapes. Attach pieces of string cheese as the tails.
- Serve bow-tie pasta with cheese and call the dish Kite Tails.
- For a candy treat, give the kids Fruit Strings (dried fruit that comes in stringy lengths).

FAVORS

- Give the kids inexpensive paper kites to take home.
- Offer the guests kite-making kits to try on their own.
- Give the guests books on how to make their own kites.

MYSTERY MAYHEM

There's no mystery to putting on a Mystery Mayhem party. All you need is a vivid imagination and a few clues on how to make it all happen. So get out your magnifying glasses—it's mystery solving time!

INVITATIONS

- Write out the party invitation on a sheet of paper and make copies for all the party guests. Then cut each copy into puzzle pieces, place in an envelope, and mail.
- Write the party details on sheets of paper using an invisible felt-tip pen kit or white crayon. Mail the papers to the guests along with the decoder pen or a dark crayon needed to reveal the invisible message.
- Send clues about the party to the guests each day, offering a little more information each time, until they can finally solve the party details mystery.

COSTUMES

- Ask the kids to wear detective outfits.
- Have the kids come as "mystery guests." Let the kids try to guess who everyone is supposed to be.

DECORATIONS

- Cut out giant question marks from black construction paper and hang them on the fences, walls, and trees.
- Write out curious questions on construction paper and place them on the table as place mats. You might also ask silly riddles, such as "Who's buried in Grant's tomb?"

GAMES

- Evidence: Buy or borrow some of the inexpensive children's books that contain "five-minute mysteries." Choose one of the mysteries and use it as the basis for this game. Collect the props mentioned in the story's plot and use them to set up the back yard as the "scene of the crime." Be sure to create lots of clues and red herrings. Gather the players and read them the mystery you've based the game on, then have the kids reenact the story and try to solve the mystery.

- Mysterious Footprints: As the guests arrive, make outlines of their shoes or footprints. When you have outlines of all the kids' feet, cut out the prints and mix them up. Have the kids race to find their "feet." Then have them try to identify whose feet are whose.
- Mystery Clue Hunt: Write out a treasure hunt using mysterious clues that lead the players from place to place. Hide the clues all over the yard and send them off in teams to find their way to the treasure.
- Mystery Map: Draw a map of the yard or park and photocopy it. Mark a path on the map for the kids to follow, looping around and around and finally leading to a mysterious treasure. Make it fun with silly landmarks, such as "Buzzard Perch" (a tree) and "Blue Lagoon" (a swimming pool). Divide the kids into teams and see who can find the treasure first.

SURPRISE INSIDE CAKE

1. Bake a sheet cake and allow it to cool.
2. Wrap small toys in plastic baggies.
3. Scoop out small holes in the cake and insert the toys.
4. Turn the cake over and frost it with white icing.
5. Make a question mark on top with chocolate icing.
6. Slice and serve to kids, making sure to warn them that there are surprises inside.

- Mystery Message: Divide the players into two teams, with one team in the front yard and the other in the back yard. Have them write mystery riddles about places in the yard, such as "You'll find a special delivery here" (the mailbox) or "This is where you go if you're bad" (the doghouse). Hide treasures at those spots. Exchange messages and yards, and have the teams try to figure out where each other's treasures are hidden.
- Mystery Star: Give each player a picture of a movie star and a black felt-tip pen. Have them disguise the person with a mustache, warts, hair, etc., without letting anyone see. Then hold the pictures up one at a time and see if anyone can recognize the star behind the disguise.

code. Have the kids then exchange messages and try to crack each other's code.
- Give the kids inexpensive masks and let them decorate them with puffy paints, sequins, feathers, glitter, and so on. When the masks are finished, have the kids put them on and try to guess who's behind the mask.

FOOD
- Make Mystery Soup. Ask each player to bring a can of soup with the label removed. Heat similar looking soups and let the kids guess the flavors.
- Serve sandwiches cut into puzzle-piece shapes.
- Unwrap a bunch of different candy bars, cut them into small bite-size pieces, and set them on a plate. Have kids try to guess what they are.

FAVORS
- Send the kids home with magnifying glasses and mystery games.
- Give the guests mystery candies—small candy bars with the outside wrapper removed—to take home and eat.

VARIATIONS
- Have a magician come to the party and dazzle the kids with tricks.

HELPFUL HINTS
- Don't make the clues too hard or the games won't be much fun.

- Scary Scavenger Hunt: Collect a bunch of silly or disgusting items and hide them around the yard. You might include such things as an empty can of cat food, a rubber snake, plastic vomit, gummy worms, and so on. Give the kids a list of the hidden items and see who can find the most.
- Which Way Did He Go? Have the kids turn around and close their eyes. Walk up behind one player and tell him or her to go and hide. When the player is hidden, have the other players open their eyes and try to find the missing player. Whoever finds the missing player first wins a prize.

ACTIVITIES
- Ask each guest to make up a mystery code and write a message using that

NATURE LOVERS PARTY

Mother Nature provides the perfect backdrop for this outdoor party. All you need is green grass to run on and sunshine to play in, then let the kids go wild in the great outdoors!

INVITATIONS

- Collect large leaves and press between two pieces of clear Contact paper. Write the party details on top in felt-tip pen and mail to guests.
- Do a leaf rubbing by placing asheet of paper over a leaf, pressing down on the paper and leaf to keep them in place, and gently rubbing a crayon lengthwise over the paper. Write the party details on the back of the paper and mail.
- Cut out a variety of colored leaves from construction paper. Write a few of the party details on each leaf, then place all the leaves in an envelope and mail. The guests must figure out the correct order of the details before they can read about the party.

- Fill the invitation's envelope with tiny plastic bugs, spiders, and ants.

CRITTER CAKE

1. Bake a sheet cake and cover it with chocolate icing.
2. Tint shredded coconut green with food coloring and sprinkle on the cake.
3. Make colorful flowers and leaves using frosting tubes.
4. Set gummy and candy bugs, worms, and spiders on top.

COSTUMES

- Ask the kids to come dressed as forest rangers, park guides, or scouts.
- Send the guests some plastic leaves and ask them to use them in a creative way as part of their costumes.
- Ask the kids to use their imaginations and dress like something in nature, such as a bug, an animal, a plant, or a tree.

DECORATIONS

- Mother Nature provides the best decorations, but you can add extra touches by

sprinkling plastic bugs, spiders, and ants on the picnic table and around the yard.

- Cut out giant colored leaves and hang them on the fence. Use smaller ones for place mats.
- Hang pictures of wildlife on the fence and walls.

GAMES

- Bug Off! Divide the group into teams and give each team a Bug House. (See Activities for instructions on building a Bug House.) Have the teams race to find as many different bugs as they can in a specific time period. Return the bugs to nature after the game is over. Be sure to have a bug book so you can identify any bugs the kids find.
- Feel the Flora and Fauna: Collect a number of items found in nature, such as a leaf, a bug, a flower, a twig, a rock, some moss, some pine needles, a pinecone, an acorn, and a bird feather. Place them in individual paper bags. Gather into a circle and pass around one bag at a time. Have the kids feel inside and try to guess what they are touching. When everyone has guessed, reveal the contents.
- The 'I Spy' Nature Walk: Make up a list of items found in nature, such as a flower, a leaf, a pine straw, and so on. Pass out the list and have the kids look around the party area or a local park for the items. Whoever finds the most items wins.
- Plant Parts: Collect parts from various plants—such as the stem of a daisy, an oak leaf, and the petal of a rose—and tape them onto a large sheet of paper. Have the kids check the chart, then try to find the matching plant in the yard. Whoever makes the most matches wins.
- Signs of Nature: Take a nature walk and have the kids pick up any items along the path that do not normally belong in nature, such as old cans, plastic bottles, paper, and so on. Give each kid a small paper bag before the walk starts. Whoever picks up the most trash wins.

ACTIVITIES

- Bug House: Give each child a half-pint milk carton with the top cut off. Place a number of small, relatively flat nature items on the table, such as flowers, leaves, stems, and so on. Cut out pieces of clear Contact paper that will fit around each container. Place the Contact paper face up in front of each child and let him or her place nature items on top. Leave enough clear space so the Contact paper will stick to the container. When the paper is decorated, have the kids wrap it around their containers to make nature-themed boxes. Then cut out circles of netting—each larger than the opening at the top of the containers—and place the netting over the top of the cartons. Secure netting with a rubber band.
- Colorful Bugs: Offer small pompoms, wiggly eyes, pipe cleaners, felt, and glue, then let the kids make their own bugs.

FOOD

- Sand and Ants: Crush four graham crackers per guest and place in individual baggies. Add a tablespoon of chocolate sprinkles to each bag and mix well.
- Let the kids create their own unique trail mix. Set out bowls of nuts, seeds, cereals, crackers, pretzels, raisins, dried fruit, marshmallows, chocolate chips, and so on. Give them plastic baggies and let them pick and choose tablespoons of mix from the various bowls.
- Give the kids edible chocolate bugs and gummy worms to eat.

VARIATIONS

- Take the kids to an arboretum or a botanical garden.

HELPFUL HINTS

- Make sure none of the kids is allergic to things in nature and beware of bees, poison oak, and other hazards.

FAVORS

- Send the nature lovers home with plastic bugs and rubber snakes.
- Give the kids magnifying glasses so they can study nature at home.
- Let the guests keep their bug catchers.
- Hand out books on such nature topics as insects, flowers, animals, and so on.

NIGHT OWLS

The dark offers a mysterious setting for a Night Owls party, where shadows dance and star-lights twinkle. Tell the kids to keep their flashlight handy—it's time for some nighttime fun!

INVITATIONS

- Find pictures of owls or draw your own on construction paper and cut them out. Write the party details on the backs and mail to the guests.
- Mail tiny flashlights to the kids in padded envelopes. Write the party details on small cards and tie them to the flashlights with string.
- Cut out and fold invitations from black construction paper. Write the party details with a glow-in-the-dark pen. On the outside of the envelopes, tell the guests to hold the card up to a light bulb for a few seconds, then turn off the lights to read the party invitation.

COSTUMES

- Have the guests come in pajamas for your nighttime party. Ask them to bring a robe and slippers, too.
- If the kids have their own flashlights, ask them to bring them along.

DECORATIONS

- Create an outside "room" by stringing up ropes between trees and fences and hanging sheets and blankets over the ropes to form walls.
- Pitch a tent for the kids to sleep in.
- Arrange the sleeping bags in a circle with the kids' heads toward the center so they can chat.
- Cut out stars from glow-in-the-dark paper and hang them from the trees.
- Cut out eyes from white construction paper; paint the eyes with glow-in-the-dark paints. Tape the eyes in pairs around the outdoor area so the kids will think that animals are watching them!
- Play a tape of animal sounds in the background.
- Give the kids mini flashlights to shine.

GAMES

- Blind Touch: Collect a number of items that are interesting to touch, such as a fuzzy slipper, a toothbrush, a sponge, a handful of fake slime, and so on. Turn out the lights and pass around the items in the dark. Let the kids feel the items and guess what they are.
- Flashlight Tag: Give the kids flashlights and let them go hide. They must try to make it back to home base without being tagged by a flashlight.
- Midnight Magic: Show the kids how to do simple magic tricks, then let them come up one at a time and perform the tricks. Darkness gives the magic tricks more power!
- Pillow Fight: Have the guests bring their own pillows to the party, then divide the kids into two teams and have a pillow fight. Place the teams on opposite sides of the yard; the kids then toss the pillows at one another and try to hit someone on the other team. Anyone who is hit is out of the game. The last team standing wins!

MILKY WAY CAKE

1. Bake a sheet cake and frost with melted Milky Way bars mixed with chocolate icing.
2. Make stars and planets using a frosting tube of white icing.
3. Before serving, stick lit mini flashlights into the cake.

- Slipper Scramble: Have the kids remove their slippers and pile them up in the middle of the yard. On the word "Go!" have the kids scramble for their own pair of slippers. The first player to put on both slippers wins the game. Or place the slippers in a paper bag and pass them around the room. Players must identify their own slippers by touch.
- Blindfold Race: Split the kids into two teams. Blindfold one kid on each team. The teams must yell out directions to their blindfolded teammate as he or she attempts to walk an obstacle course made of soft items like pillows and blankets. Once the blindfolded racer reaches

onto the light, then shine the light against a flat surface in the dark. Watch the image appear!

FOOD
- Offer a cereal buffet for a late-night snack or early-morning breakfast. Set out bowls of different cereals in a long row, each with its own serving spoons. Supply lots of milk at the end of the table. Let the kids move down the buffet line with their own bowls and scoop out whatever cereals they want.
- S'mores are fun for a midnight snack. Heat marshmallows over a fire or gas flame, press between two graham crackers with a piece of chocolate bar inside. Or have a bowl of S'mores cereal.

FAVORS
- Give the kids decorated socks to wear home.
- Find nightcaps at the novelty store and give them to the kids.
- Let the kids keep the mini flashlights from the party.

VARIATIONS
- Make a trip to the local planetarium or set up a telescope in the yard.

HELPFUL HINTS
- Some kids are afraid of the dark, so make sure everyone has a flashlight handy.

the end, he or she races back and gives another teammate the blindfold. The first team to finish wins.

ACTIVITIES
- Glow-in-the-Dark Art: Let the kids draw or paint on white paper with glow-in-the-dark pens or paints. When they're finished, turn the lights off and watch the pictures appear!
- Batman Signals: Let the kids make their own Batman Signals using construction paper and flashlights. Have the kids cut out different designs from black construction paper, making sure each design is a little larger than the lens of their flashlight. Tape the cut-out design

OLYMPIC GOLD

Go for the gold with this backyard Olympic Gold party! Set up plenty of fun challenges, test the kids' skills, and let them win medals for their country. Let the games begin!

INVITATIONS

- Cut out award ribbons from red, white, and blue ribbon fabric. Attach a gold seal to the top, cut the bottom into an inverted V shape, and write the party details in permanent felt-tip pen on the front of the ribbon. Mail to the guests.
- Collect pictures of former Olympic winners from sports magazines or trading cards, glue onto folded cards, and write party details inside.

COSTUMES

- Ask the guests to come dressed in athletic outfits that are comfortable and flexible.
- Have the kids come dressed as their favorite Olympic medal winner.
- Have each kid come dressed as an athlete from a different country.

THREE MEDAL CAKE

1. Bake three round cakes.
2. Frost with three different, bright colored frostings.
3. Attach ribbons on top to simulate Olympic medals.

DECORATIONS

- Buy small trophies to set on the table at each place setting. Use a large trophy as a centerpiece.
- Hang medals and prize ribbons from the fence and trees.
- Buy or make a collection of country flags and hang them on the fence. Make place mats from flags of different countries and assign a country to each contestant.
- Hang Olympic posters on the walls and fences.

GAMES

• Balance Board: Wrap an eight- to ten-foot length of 2-by-4 board tightly in an old blanket or sheet; use electrical tape to keep this padding from slipping. Balance the board on a couple of bricks. Have the contestants walk across the board one at a time. Anyone who falls off is out. Increase the difficulty of the walk with each round by having the kids walk sideways, backwards, with their eyes closed, and so on.

• Blind Snakes: Set up a number of sprinklers in between a starting line and a finish line. Have the kids try to run from one end to the other without getting sprayed. Have one of the kids control the faucet, turning it on and off at random. Award ribbons to the kids who play the longest without getting wet.

• Body Mechanics: Design a series of athletic events the contestants must perform, such as hopping on one foot ten times, walking ten steps backwards without looking, walking like a crab, skipping backwards, jumping over a hurdle, throwing a ball up in the air while turning around and catching it, and so on. Award ribbons to the best athletes in each event.

• Cross Step: Draw a ten-by-ten-foot grid on the sidewalk or patio with chalk. Have each player stand on a different square. One at a time, each contestant must move to a new square after crossing out the square he or she was formerly standing in. The trick is that the players cannot step into a square that is occupied or crossed out. If a player cannot move to a new square, he or she is out. The game continues until only one player is left.

• Decathlon: Create ten different challenges for the contestants to perform, such as running around the block as fast as they can, seeing how far they can throw a ball, shooting ten baskets, hitting a baseball, swimming ten laps, jumping through a hoop, and so on. Give points to the players based on how well they do in each event, then award prizes to the players who receive the best combined scores for all the events.

- Gymnastics: Set out a pad or mattress. Have the kids do stunts on the pad, such as somersaults, rolls, cartwheels, knee-walks, headstands, handstands, and so on.
- Obstacle Course: Set a series of obstacles and have the players run through them. Include such things as crawling through a tunnel, climbing over a table, wiggling under a carpet, and so on. Award prizes to the kids who complete the course in the best times.

ACTIVITIES

- Give the kids squares of white fabric, approximately two feet by one foot, attached to a small stick to form a flag. Set out felt-tip pens and let the kids color the fabric and design their own national flags.
- Divide the players into teams and have them design their own Olympic challenges for each other.

VARIATIONS

- Take the kids to a sporting event.

HELPFUL HINTS

- Make sure everyone wins at some event so there are no losers.

FOOD

- Make finger snacks for the kids to eat on the go, such as finger sandwiches, cheese and crackers, cut-up fruits, and nuts.
- Give the kids power bars to keep them going. Let them wash the snacks down with sports drinks.
- As a treat, offer chocolate gold coin "medals."

FAVORS

- Send the kids home with ribbons and trophies.
- Give the kids posters of Olympic winners.
- Hand out chocolate gold coin "medals."

OUTDOOR THEATER PARTY

There's nothing like theater alfresco! After all, all the world's a stage, even the backyard. All it takes is a little creativity and imagination. Actors take your marks—it's time for the show!

INVITATIONS
- Make giant tickets from construction paper. Write the party details where the information normally goes on the tickets. Mail to guests.
- Send a mask to each of the guests with the party details written on the back.
- Buy postcard playbills—or make your own—and send them to the guests. Write the party information on the back.

COSTUMES
- Ask the kids to come in a favorite movie or theater costume.
- Have the kids dress specifically for a selected play, with assigned parts for all the actors.

DECORATIONS
- Set up a stage for the featured production by setting a platform of wood on a brick foundation, about a foot off the ground.
- Hang sheets and blankets from ropes strung to trees to make curtains.
- Set up chairs or picnic benches facing the stage for the audience.
- Hang posters of famous movie stars or theater productions on the fence and walls.

- Cut out silver stars and place them around the stage and curtains. Use them for place markers at the table.
- Play music from Broadway shows in the background.

GAMES
- Academy Awards: Have your own Academy Awards. Let the kids nominate their favorite movies, actors, and scenes from movies for the awards, then let them vote and see who wins an Oscar!

- Famous Scenes: Divide the kids into teams and have each team take turns acting out scenes from famous movies. Let the other teams try to guess the name of the movie. Award points for correct answers.
- Movie Trivia: Think up questions regarding recent movies that the kids have seen and write them down on slips of paper. Divide the kids into several teams. Let each team draw a slip from the bag and try to answer the question. Teams receive one point for each correct answer.

ACTIVITIES

- Put on a Play: Go to the library and choose a simple play for the kids—or create your own using a favorite children's book. Photocopy the scripts for the actors and let them learn their parts. An easy way for the actors to read their lines is to glue the scripts to the back of props.
- Costumes and Props: After the kids read over their parts, let them create their

own costumes using old clothes from the thrift shop or large sheets of crepe paper. They can also make the props for the play.
- Make-Up Makeover: Before the play starts, have the actors do one another's make-up. Provide a variety of make-up items, lots of wet towels for handy clean-up, and mirrors for checking the progress of the make-up.

THEATER TICKET CAKE
1. Make a sheet cake and frost it with white icing.
2. Using a chocolate frosting tube, write in the details to make the cake look like a theater ticket.
3. Decorate around the cake with colored popcorn.

FAVORS

- Send the kids home with an inexpensive video.
- Give the guests tickets to a local movie theater.
- Hand out theatrical make-up for the kids to try at home.
- Let the guests keep their costumes.

- Drive-In Movie: Create a Drive-In Movie by bringing the TV outside, setting chairs up around it, and playing a video when night falls.

VARIATIONS

- Take the kids to a matinee play at the local children's theater.

FOOD

- Refreshment Counter: Set up a snack counter for distributing popcorn, candy and sodas.
- Let the kids make their own popcorn and lemonade, if you prefer, as one of the party activities.

HELPFUL HINTS

- If some of the kids are shy, give them the less-demanding parts and let them read from their scripts instead of having to memorize their lines.

PARK RANGER

Let the Park Ranger be your guide to outdoor fun and games. Set up a tent at your favorite local, state, or national park, then watch out for bears as the kids blaze the trails!

INVITATIONS

- Cut out teddy bears from coloring books or draw them on construction paper. Write the party details on the backs and mail to the guests.
- Get postcards from the park and write the party details on the back.
- Make park ranger badges by covering tagboard stars with foil. Write the guests' names and the party details on the badges using permanent felt-tip pen.

TEDDY BEAR CAKE

1. Bake two round chocolate cakes and eight chocolate cupcakes.
2. Lay the two round cakes on the table, one beside the other, to form the bear's head and body.
3. Set two cupcakes on either side of the head to form ears, two on either side of the upper body to form arms, two on either side of the lower body to form legs, and one in the center of the head for the nose.
4. Use frosting tubes and candy to make eyes, nostrils, mouth, and paws.

COSTUMES

- Ask the kids to dress as park rangers in khaki shorts or long pants and white or khaki shirts. Give everyone ranger badges when they arrive.
- Encourage the guests to wear hiking boots and backpacks for the trail walks.

DECORATIONS

- Spread checkered tablecloths on the picnic tables. Set the table with tin plates and cups.

Another option is to simply have an adult act like a bear without the costume.

- Feeling Nature: Collect a number of nature items and put each one in a separate paper bag. Have the guests sit in a circle. Pass the bags around the circle and let each kid feel inside the bags and try to guess what the objects are. After all the items have been identified, open the bags and see who got the most right.
- Lost! Blindfold one of the players and turn him or her around in a circle. The player must find his or her way back to camp area from a short distance away, while the others make distracting animals noises. Once the player reaches the camp area, or gets hopelessly lost, blindfold a different player. The player who reaches camp in the shortest amount of time wins.

- Hang park posters around the picnic area.
- Cut out large bears from brown tagboard and set them up near the picnic tables.

GAMES

- Bear Hunt: Put one of the adults in a rented bear costume somewhere on the trail. Tell the rangers they have to make it from the start of the trail to the end, without being caught and tagged by the bear, which is hiding along the way!

- Park Bingo: Make bingo cards and write down park items in each of the squares, such as an acorn, a yellow leaf, a dead bug, a smooth stone, a pine needle, a bird feather, a wildflower, and so on. Mix up the order of the items and use some different items on each of the cards. Give a card to each ranger and have the kids search the area for the items on their cards. The first one to collect five items in a row wins the game.
- Trail Blazer: Divide the group into two teams and have them take a hike on different paths. As they walk, have them make arrows and other markers using sticks and rocks for the other team to follow. When both teams return, have them switch paths and see if they can follow the other team's trail.

ACTIVITIES
- Camp Collage: Have the kids collect nature items on a trail walk. Bring the items to the picnic table and spread them out. Distribute large sheets of paper to each ranger to create a collage using the items on the table and some glue.

VARIATIONS
- Camp out all night at the park.

HELPFUL HINTS
- Watch out for snakes, poison oak, and other hazards. Pair the kids using the buddy system so they don't get lost.

- Get a scout book and teach the kids different skills, such as how to tie knots, find water, make a fire, build a lean-to, treat a snake bite, use a compass, and so on.

FOOD
- Give the kids trail mix and a bottle of water to take along on the hikes.
- Make telescope sandwiches by cutting the crust off bread slices, placing a slice of cheese or bologna on the bread, and rolling it into a telescope. Secure with a toothpick.

FAVORS
- Give the kids compasses, small telescopes, and maps to take home.
- Buy inexpensive nature books about insects, plants, animals, or birds, to give to the departing rangers.

PARTY PICNIC

Have a portable Party Picnic and take your fun and games with you. You can set up the picnic in the backyard, take it to the park or playground, or head to the campground and spend the day enjoying food and fun.

INVITATIONS
- Send the kids the party details written on paper picnic napkins.
- Fold up tiny tablecloths with the party information written inside and mail to guests.
- Cut out giant ants from black construction paper, write the party details in white ink, and mail to the guests.
- Fold brown construction paper into cards and decorate them with felt-tip pen to look like wicker baskets. Write the party details inside and mail to guests.
- Enclose plastic ants in the envelope for an extra surprise.

COSTUMES
- Have the kids wear shorts and tops if the weather is warm, sweats and athletic gear if it's cool.

DECORATIONS
- Find a large checkered tablecloth for your party and lay it on the table or on the ground for the picnic.
- Set colorful paper plates at each place setting. Write the guests' names around the rims of the plates.

- Set a picnic basket filled with fruit, cheese, and crackers in the center of the tablecloth.
- Cut out ants from black construction paper or buy plastic ants from the toy store. Place the ants all around the picnic area.

GAMES
- Crazy Croquet: Use your old croquet set in this new version of the game. Stick the hoops in the ground at varying dis-

tances, but make things challenging by putting the hoops in holes, on mounds, near water, and so on. Have the kids swing their mallets with their nondominant hand or close their eyes before they strike the ball. Instead of croquet balls, use tennis balls, golf balls, Ping-Pong balls, and so on.

- Frisbee Tag: Give everyone a Frisbee and spread the kids out on the field. Have the players try to tag one another with the Frisbees. Anyone who gets tagged is out of the game. Play until only one person is left.
- Pie-Eating Contest: Set a bunch of mini pies on the picnic table, making sure you have one for each player. On the word "Go!" have the kids race to eat their pies without using their hands. The first one to finish a pie wins a prize. You can also have a drinking contest by filling small bowls with punch and having the contestants lap them up without using their hands.

DIRT AND WORMS CUPCAKES

1. Bake chocolate cupcakes and frost with chocolate icing.
2. Cover with chocolate cookie crumbs or chocolate sprinkles.
3. Stick a gummy worm into the top of the cupcake. Let half the worm hang out over the side.
4. Stick a plastic flower in the center and serve to the kids.

- Seed Spit: Set out bowls three feet away from each contestant. Have players sit down with a slice of watermelon, eat the melon, and try to spit the seeds into the bowls. The player with the most seeds in the bowl wins the game.
- Taster's Choice: Have the kids sit around the picnic table and close their eyes. Pass around a picnic food—such as a piece of cheese, a cracker, a piece of fruit, and so on—and have the kids try to guess what they are eating.

ACTIVITIES

- Give the kids small picnic baskets and let them color the baskets with paints, felt-tip pens, or puffy paints. Let the

kids take the baskets home when they are dry for their own little picnics.

- After the big picnic meal, have everyone lie on their backs on the tablecloth and stare at the clouds. Tell the kids to describe what they see in the clouds. See who can find the weirdest and funniest shapes in the clouds.

FOOD

- Provide a variety of picnic foods—cut-up sandwiches, olives, cheese cubes, watermelon, dip and chips, fruit salad, macaroni salad, and so on.
- Offer drinks in plastic bottles that the kids can carry around with them.

FAVORS

- Give the kids a collection of plastic bugs to take home.
- Pass out butterfly nets to go.
- Give the guests mini picnic baskets for their own picnics.
- Send the kids home with their own Frisbees.

VARIATIONS

- Have a tailgate picnic in the back of a truck at a ballgame.

HELPFUL HINTS

- Check to see if any of the kids have outdoor or food allergies before the picnic.

SILLY SPORTS

How do you host a Silly Sports party? Just take the kids' favorite games and give them a twist. Any sport is bound to turn out silly using a different type of ball, a different course, and a different set of rules!

INVITATIONS

- Buy a pack of inexpensive sports cards. Write the party details on the backs of the cards and mail to the guests.
- Write the party details on mini Frisbees and send them in padded envelopes to the guests.
- With a permanent felt-tip pen, write the party information on Ping-Pong balls. Stuff them in padded envelopes or small boxes and send to the guests.
- Make sports banners out of construction paper, write the party details on the front, and mail to the guests.

SILLY SPORTS CAKE

1. Bake a sheet cake and frost it with chocolate icing.
2. Tint shredded coconut green with food coloring and sprinkle over the cake.
3. Set up a silly game by placing football, soccer, baseball, and basketball plastic sports figures on the cake.

COSTUMES

- Ask the kids to wear a sports jersey to the party.
- Have the guests wear comfortable clothes, athletic suits, or T-shirts and shorts.
- Suggest the kids wear some kind of silly sports costume, such as a baseball hat with a football shirt, golf pants with a skateboard shirt, or basketball shoes with a swimsuit.

GAMES

- Weird Baseball: Play a game of baseball without baseballs! Substitute other items for the baseballs, such as tennis balls, Ping-Pong balls, Nerf balls, sponges, sock balls, soccer balls, and beach balls. Alternate the balls constantly so that everyone has to hit a different type of ball!
- Birdless Badminton: Play a game of badminton without a birdie by substituting something silly instead, such as a Ping-Pong ball, a high-bounce rubber ball, a sock ball, a sponge, a tennis ball, and so on.
- Blindfold Basketball: Play a game of stunt basketball, such as "Horse" or "Around the World." The twist is that each time the players shoot the ball, they must close their eyes!
- Crooked Croquet: Set up a croquet course using odd objects instead of croquet hoops. You might try a shoebox, two paper plates, a pair of shoes separated by a short distance, a propped-open book, a circle of rope, and so on. Also use weird substitutes for the croquet sticks, such as broom handles and baseball bats, and silly stuff for the balls, such as stuffed toys, soup cans, small pillows, oranges, and so on.
- Funny Flag Football: Instead of playing regular football, play flag football using colorful flags tucked into the back pockets or sides of the kids' pants.

DECORATIONS

- Set out sports memorabilia around the playing field, the table, and the fence and walls.
- Hang sports banners and make up silly sports slogans, such as "Slam Dunk Ping-Pong" and "Crooked Croquet."
- Make a large sports card place mat for each guest, using a blowup of a school yearbook photograph. Laminate the mats with clear Contact paper and set around the table.

- Golf Pool: Play a game of pool using golf or Ping-Pong balls, or play a game of golf using tennis or Ping-Pong balls.
- Hoops and Scoops: Play basketball set to dance music, so that the kids have to dribble and shoot the ball in time to the beats.
- Lazy Lawn Darts: Play a game of lawn darts while sitting in a chair instead of standing up. Or play a game of regular darts while sitting down.
- People Ball: Play a game of baseball using people as balls! Have the pitcher shove the people ball to the batter, who shoves the people ball out to the field while he or she runs for first base. The outfielders must catch the people ball and run him or her over to the base to put the runner out.
- Street Hockey: Play a game of hockey on the patio, driveway, or court. Let the kids hit the puck with sticks into goals made from old tires or cardboard boxes.
- Super Soccer: Play a game of soccer using a tennis or beach ball instead of a soccer ball.

VARIATIONS
- Take the kids out to a real ball game.

HELPFUL HINTS
- Be sure to supervise the kids at play, since they're trying new versions of favorite games and may be unsure of what to do.

ACTIVITIES
- Have the kids design their own silly sports jerseys by decorating white T-shirts with felt-tip pens, decals, and puffy paints.
- Divide the kids into two teams and have them create a silly sport for the other team to play.

FOOD
- Serve the sports fans ballpark food—hot dogs, corn dogs, and nachos.
- Give the kids peanuts and popcorn for a between-meal treat.
- Keep sports drinks handy for the athletes.

FAVORS
- Send the kids home with sports cards, jerseys, banners, and other sports accessories.
- Give the guests the balls from the party.

SKATE-AWAY

Host a skating party in your neighborhood park or driveway and let the kids show off their in-line skating and skateboarding skills. Teach them a few tricks, play a few games, and everyone will skate away happy!

INVITATIONS

- Buy pairs of long white shoelaces. Write the party details in felt-tip pen on the laces, tie them into bows, and mail to the skaters.
- Cut out pictures of skates or skateboards and write the party details on top. Punch holes in the skates and lace them up with thin red or black licorice strings. For the skateboard, tape on Lifesaver candies for the wheels.
- Buy skateboard decals at the sports store and include them with the party invitations.

COSTUMES

- Ask the kids to come dressed in skating outfits. Have them bring their kneepads, elbow pads, helmets, and other accessories. Rent extra pads from the skating store, if you prefer.
- Have the guests come dressed as skateboarders with oversized pants and baggy shirts.

DECORATIONS

- Hang posters of Olympic skaters around the skating area.

- Borrow old skates from the skating rink and set them around as props.
- Borrow vintage skateboards from older neighborhood kids to use as props.
- Cut out pictures of skateboarders from skateboard magazines and hang them around the area.
- Place the plates of food on top of skateboards.
- Play upbeat skating music in the background.

GAMES

- Blind Skate: Have the kids close their eyes and try to skate one at a time across the designated area. Set up obstacles and have a partner lead them around.
- Skateboard Finals: Design a series of skateboard stunts and have the kids play follow the leader. If someone messes up a stunt he or she is out of the game. Play until only one skater is left. Possible stunts include skating down a ramp, over a board, up a sidewalk, down a step, and so on.
- Skater's Olympics: Set up a series of obstacles for the skaters to maneuver around, such as a chair, a series of cones, through a large box, under a table, and so on. Time the skaters as

they go through the course one at a time. Award prizes to the skaters with the best times.

- Skate Race: Divide the players into two teams lined up in two rows. On the word "Go!" have the first two players race from one side of the skating area to the other and back again, then tag the next players to continue the race. The team that finishes first wins.
- Skate Tag: Play a game of tag on skates!

SKATEBOARD CAKE

1. Bake a sheet cake. When cool, round the edges with a knife.
2. Bake four cupcakes.
3. Frost the cake and cupcakes with different-colored icing.
4. Add skateboard decorations and details to the cake with tubes of icing, sprinkles, and small candy.
5. Slice the cupcake tops off and press them into the sides of the cake to make wheels.

For a skating cake, make a sheetcake, frost to resemble a rink, and set small plastic skaters on top.

ACTIVITIES

• Let the kids made their own skating decals. Let them draw designs on small squares of white tagboard using felt-tip pens. Cover the paper with a sheet of clear Contact paper that is cut a little larger than the white squares so the edges will be sticky. The kids can then stick their new decals on their skateboards or skates.

FOOD

• Give the kids sports drinks and power bars to eat when they take breaks from skating.

FAVORS

• Give the kids skating decals to take home.
• Offer skateboard shirts to keep.
• Hand out skating magazines to the guests.
• Give the kids wristbands and kneepads to take home.

VARIATIONS

• Take the kids to the skating rink or a skateboard park and let them practice their skills.

HELPFUL HINTS

• Make sure everyone is well-padded so no one gets hurt.

SPACE: THE FINAL FRONTIER

For the ultimate outdoor party, head for the final frontier—outer space. Host your party at night when the stars are bright and take a journey into the unknown. This party's out of this world!

INVITATIONS
- Buy a package of glow-in-the-dark stars and planets. Write the party details in permanent felt-tip pen on several of the stars and planets and mail to guests.
- Photocopy a current night sky chart. Rename the stars with the guests' names, then give instructions so each guest can reach the party star.

- Send the invitations via homemade spaceships cut from construction paper, or use small plastic spaceships to send your message.
- Write the party details on black paper using a white paint pen. Use glue-on or stick-on stars as added decoration.

COSTUMES
- Ask the kids to come wearing space suits, alien costumes, or Star Trek and Star Wars outfits.
- Send the guests stick-on stars with the invitations. Ask them to stick the stars on their clothes and faces in a creative way before they come to the party.

GALAXY CAKE
1. Bake a round cake and frost it with orange-tinted icing to make it look like the sun.
2. Poke thin wooden skewers of varying lengths into large and small marshmallows. Insert the other end of sticks into the cake to make planets. Begin with a small marshmallow set close to the sun for Mercury, and assorted large and small marshmallows for the rest of the planets.
3. Paint the marshmallows with food coloring to make the planets more colorful.

GAMES

- Alien Invaders: When the guests arrive, attach the same amount of star stickers on each kid's clothes. Once everyone has arrived, pass out cards to each player, with half the cards marked "alien" and half marked "earthling." During the party, the aliens must collect speci-mens—the stuck-on stars—from the earthlings without being caught. If any alien is caught removing a sticker, he or she must give the earthling who caught them a sticker. The player with the most stickers at the end of the party wins.

- Flying Saucers: Cut out flying saucers—each the size of a large plate—from heavy tagboard or cardboard. Cut a three- or four-inch hole in the middle of the saucer. Have the kids paint the saucers and decorate them with stick-ers. Then line up the kids and have them toss their saucers like Frisbees across the galaxy (the yard). Whoever sends a saucer flying the farthest wins a prize.

- Planet Earthywood: Seat three players at a table while the rest of the guests sit on the other side to form an audi-ence. Place a bell or a squeaky toy in the front of each player. Read prepared questions about earth and space from index cards; any player who knows the answer rings their bell or squeaks their toy. If it's a correct answer, he or she gets a point. If it's a wrong answer, another player gets a chance to answer. After five points are reached, award a

DECORATIONS

- Cut out stars from glow-in-the-dark paper (or paint the stars with glow-in-the-dark paint) and stick them around the fences, house, and trees. Add a few planets and spaceships, too.
- Get out your Star Wars and Star Trek toys and use them as a centerpiece for the table.
- Cover the table with black paper and place white stars on it with glow-in-the-dark paint or stickers. Make paper plate planets and name each one after a guest, such as "Planet Tiffany" and "Planet Jason."
- Play space-movie music in the background.

prize and exchange the contestants for a new set of players.

- Star Search: Give each player a chart of the current night sky, a pen, and a small flashlight. Have them lie on their backs, looking up at the sky. Tell them they are to find as many of the constellations as they can and check them off on their sky charts. Whoever finds the most constellations in a limited period of time wins.

ACTIVITIES

- Sky Rockets: Get a book from the library or bookstore on how to build small rockets. Collect the materials needed, then let the kids make their own Sky Rockets. Launch the rockets to see which one goes up the farthest. For a nonchemical alternative, launch slingshot rockets by shooting plastic ships from slingshots.
- Space Ship: Create a giant spaceship from a large appliance box. Let the kids paint it to look like one of the U.S. spaceships, then let them climb in and pretend they're blasting off into space.

VARIATIONS

- Take the kids to the planetarium for a sightseeing trip to outer space.

HELPFUL HINTS

- Choose a clear night for your party so the kids can see the stars and enjoy the night air.

FOOD

- Serve the space explorers freeze-dried astronaut foods, such as soup, beef stew, and ice cream, all of which are available at camping stores.
- Cut out star-shaped sandwiches using a cookie cutter.
- Make Tang—the drink of astronauts—to serve the kids.

FAVORS

- Give the kids space or star books to take home.
- Give the guests toy binoculars or telescopes to study the sky.
- Buy some inexpensive space-related toys, such as spaceships, stars, alien figures, and so on, and hand them out to the kids.

TAG TEAM

It takes teamwork to put on a good party and teamwork to have a great time at this party! Here are some games of tag that will keep your party moving all afternoon.

INVITATIONS
- Write the party details on luggage tags to get your Tag Team party going. Mail to the guests.
- Make a finish line out of yellow crepe paper or ribbon, write the party details on it, and mail to the guests in a large envelope.
- Create your own starting flags by cutting out squares of white fabric. Draw a large "GO!" on one side and add party details around the edges. Attach a short stick and mail to the guests.

COSTUMES
- Ask the kids to wear racing clothes, athletic outfits, or shorts and T-shirts so they can move quickly.
- Make T-shirts for two teams by using two different colors for background, such as red and blue. Draw on team names, such as "Sharks" and "Whales," and players' names with felt-tip pens or puffy paints. Give the shirts to the kids when they arrive at the party.

DECORATIONS
- Buy large sheets of tagboard or construction paper in a variety of colors or in the colors of the two teams. Write

cheerleading slogans on the signs, such as "Go Sharks!" or "Whales Rule!" Hang them up around the yard.
- Set the table with paper and plastic plates and cups in the team colors. Make place mats in the shape of racing flags.
- Play sports music in the background.

GAMES
- Bank Robber: Divide the group into two teams. Give a paper bag of gold coins to one player on each team and have the teams stand at opposite ends of the yard. On the word "Go!" the bag holders must try to keep anyone on the oppos-

ing team from touching their bag of gold coins. The bag holders can pass the bag to other players on their team, but if the bag is touched, the opposing team gets to eat one of the gold coins in the bag. The bag is then returned and the game continues until only one team has any gold coins left.

- Grab the Loot: Divide the kids equally into two teams on opposite sides of the yard. Place a small prize—such as a candy bar or a pack of gum—in the middle of the yard between the two teams. Give the members of each team a number—one, two, three, and so on—then repeat the same numbers for the other team. When the referee calls a number, the two players with that number must run to the center of the field, try to grab the loot, and run back without being caught by the other player. Continually

put out new pieces of loot and call new numbers. The team with the most loot at the end of the game wins.

- Loose Goose: Have the players sit in a large circle, facing in toward the middle. Tape a feather or a piece of construction paper to the back of each player. Choose one player to be the goose. The goose walks around the outside of the circle and grabs the feather from one of the seated players. That player must jump up and try to run and tag the goose before the goose runs all the way around the circle and sits in the empty spot. If the player can't tag the goose, he or she becomes the goose.

- Octopus Tag: One player is chosen as the octopus and must stand in between two lines of players on opposite sides of the yard. Players try to cross the yard to

OCTOPUS CAKE
1. Make a round cake and sixty-four mini cupcakes.
2. Frost with green-tinted icing.
3. Set eight cupcakes around the cake to begin the legs of the octopus. Add seven more cupcakes to each of the initial eight to finish the legs.
4. Set two large marshmallows on the round cake to make the eyes. Color the eyes with tube icing. Make a mouth out of red licorice. Sprinkle on colorful candies for spots.

the other side without getting tagged by the octopus. If the octopus tags someone, he or she joins the octopus in the center by holding hands. They continue to try to capture more players until everyone is part of the octopus.

- Pick Pocket Tag: Put a strip of cloth in each player's back pocket. Have the players try to grab each other's strips without having their own strip taken. The player with the most cloth strips wins the game.

ACTIVITIES

- Have the kids make their own racing flags. Give them two-by-three-feet squares of white cloth stapled to a two-foot-long stick. Let the kids design and color their flags using felt-tip pens or puffy paints.

- Let the kids make their own team jerseys. Give everyone a white T-shirt and iron-on crayons to decorate their shirts. When the kids are finished, iron the designs to make the colors last.
- Divide the kids into two teams and have them make up their own version of tag to play with the other team.

FOOD

- Have a Peanut Butter and Jelly Race. Give the kids two slices of bread, a plastic knife, and a paper plate. Have them race to make their sandwiches, reminding them they must eat what they make.
- Serve the kids sports drinks in between games.
- Give the kids gold coins for special treats.

FAVORS

- Give the kids pocket games to take home so they can keep playing.
- Buy inexpensive game books and send them home with the kids.
- Give the guests racing flags and let them keep their new T-shirts.

VARIATIONS

- Combine relay games with the tag games to create your own games.

HELPFUL HINTS

- Change the teams around every now and then so the same players don't keep winning.

TEAM PLAYERS

It's amazing how a group of kids playing together can make a party fun! All it takes is Team Players—the kids can't wait to share the fun with their teammates!

INVITATIONS

- Put together a group collage of the invited guests by cutting out school photos and assembling them together. Draw cartoon bodies of the kids playing together, photocopy, write the party details on the back, and mail to the guests.
- Send each guest a white piece of paper, approximately three-by-three inches square. On one side write the party information. On the other side, ask the guests to draw a picture of themselves and bring it to the party. When the guests arrive, tape the pictures together to make a giant paper quilt of the team. Hang it up so everyone can see it.

COSTUMES

- Have the kids dress in athletic wear, sweat suits, or shorts and T-shirts.
- Give the kids T-shirts with their teams' names and their personal names written on the backs of the shirts in felt-tip pen or puffy paints.

TEAM PLAYERS CAKE

1. Bake a sheet cake and frost it with white or chocolate icing.
2. Cut out head shots of the guests and cover both sides with clear Contact paper to protect them.
3. Place the heads on the cake and draw stick figure bodies under them with tubes of icing.

DECORATIONS

- Blow up pictures of the kids into posters and hang them up.
- Have the kids make life-sized body portraits by lying down on large sheets of white paper and tracing each other's outlines. Then let them color in their features and clothes. Cut out the images and hang them on a wall.

• Write the teams' names on a white paper tablecloth and cover the table with it. Have the guests sign their names on the tablecloth.

GAMES

• Bubble Bust: Give each kid a vial of soap solution and a bubble wand. Divide the kids into two teams and have them blow, catch, and pop bubbles. See which team can blow the most bubbles, the biggest bubble, and float the highest bubble.

• Capture the Flag: Divide the kids into two teams. Make two different flags, one for each team, and set the flags in the middle of the yard. Line the teams up on either side of the flags and have them try to get their team's flag without being grabbed by the other side. The first team to capture their flag and return to their side of the yard wins.

• Crossfire: Divide the kids into three teams. Have two teams stand in two lines about eight feet apart and give each kid a ball. Have the third team try to run through the line without getting hit by the balls; any player who gets hit is out. Repeat, changing teams, until only one team is left standing.

• Drag the Body: Divide the group into two teams. Give each team a blanket. Have one player from each team lie down on the blanket. The teams must drag the body on the blanket from one end of the yard to the other. Whoever crosses the finish line first wins the game.

• Four-Corner Volleyball: Make a large X on the ground using chalk or ropes. Divide the kids into four teams and have them stand in the four sections formed by the X. Play a game of volleyball among the four teams using a single ball.

• Free-For-All-Frisbee: Divide the group into two teams and give all the kids mini Frisbees—a different color for each team. Place a box in the center of the yard and have the teams line up on either side, several yards from the box. On the word "Go!" they are to try to land as many Frisbees at they can in the box. The team with the most Frisbees in the box wins.

- Kill the Cockroach: Divide the players into two teams. Line them up, one in front of the other and set an odd object in front of the first players in line. They must kick the object across the yard and across the finish line to win a point for their team. Kick things like a pillow, an empty can, a sock, and so on.
- Knock It Off: Set up ten weird items that can be knocked over by a ball—such as an empty can, a box, a doll, and so on—and place them in a row. Divide the players into two teams and line them up, one in front of the other. The first two players must roll a ball across the yard and try to knock over one of the items selected by the referee to win a point for their team. Next players in line continue, until all items have been knocked over.
- Towel Toss: Divide the players into two teams. Give each team a large beach towel and a ball. The teams form a circle around their towel and hold onto the ends. The ball is placed in the middle and the teams must try to bounce the ball up

and down without letting it drop off the towel. The team that can do the most bounces without dropping the ball wins.

ACTIVITIES
- Let the kids design their own team logos, names, banners, and jerseys with permanent felt-tip pens, puffy paints, and iron-on crayons and decals.
- Have the kids design a team game that they can play.

FOOD
- Give the teams sports drinks and power bars to keep their energy up.
- If it's hot outside, provide plenty of Popsicles for refreshment.
- Offer a sandwich bar with plenty of bread and fillings.

FAVORS
- Give the kids a ball to take home.
- Hand out game books to go.

VARIATIONS
- Take the kids to some team games or sports so they can see teamwork in action.

HELPFUL HINTS
- Mix up the teams so that everyone has a chance to win.

WET AND WILD

A Wet and Wild party is perfect for those hot days when the kids need to cool off. Don't worry about traveling to a swimming pool or lake—for this party, all you need is lots and lots of water!

INVITATIONS
- Send the guests little baggies of blue-tinted water. Tie the party details to the bags and mail in boxes or hand deliver.
- Mail out postcards of beach scenes with the party details written on the backs.
- Write the party details along the frames of inexpensive sunglasses. Wrap in bubble plastic and mail in padded envelopes to the guests.
- Fill baggies with a little sand, write the party details on the baggies with permanent felt-tip pen, and mail to guests.

COSTUMES
- Tell the kids the wear their bathing suits and bring along sandals, towels, and beach toys.
- Provide the guests with sunglasses, suntan lotion, and hats.

DECORATIONS
- Hang fishnets on the fence and over the picnic table.
- Cut out brightly colored construction-paper fish in various sizes and hang them around the yard. Use some of the fish for place mats.
- Cut out giant drops of water from blue construction paper and hang them from the fence.
- Serve the food in plastic sand pails and let the kids eat with plastic shovels.

GAMES
- Bucket Brigade: Divide the group into two teams and line them up in two parallel rows. Give the first players on each

team a bucket. Set a tub of water next to each of the first players in line and an empty tub at the end of each line. On the word "Go!" the first players are to dip their buckets into the tubs of water and pass the buckets down the row of players. The last player then dumps the water into an empty tub and passes the bucket back. The first team to empty the full tub wins the game.

- Keep It Dry: Turn on as many sprinklers as possible for this game. Line up two teams on one side of the yard and give each kid a sheet of colored tissue paper. The players must run through the sprinklers while trying not to get their paper wet. The team with the most dry papers wins the game.
- Sinking Ship: Divide the players into two teams and place them in two lines. Give the first players on each team a pie plate full of water. Players must pass the pie plate over their heads to the player behind them until the pie pan reaches the end of the line. The team with the most water left in the pie plate wins.
- Splash Maker: This is a version of Duck, Duck, Goose that's played with water.

FISH BOWL CAKE
1. Bake a round cake and frost it with blue-tinted icing.
2. Swirl waves on the side of the cake with icing tinted a darker blue.
3. Set gummy fish on top of the cake.

Seat the kids in a circle. Give one player a cup of water and have him or her walk around the outside of the circle. After a few moments, the player is to dump the water on one of the sitting players, then run around the outside and try to get back to the open space before the wet player catches him or her.

- Tug-of-Water War: Fill a kiddy pool with water. Divide the kids into two teams and place each team on opposite sides of the kiddy pool. Place a rope between the teams for a tug-of-war, then have them try to pull one another into the water.
- Water Bomb Toss: Divide the kids into pairs and have them stand about two

ACTIVITIES
- Let the kids take a break from the active water play by painting with watercolors.
- Make an Ocean in a Bottle by filling a clear plastic pop bottle with water, adding blue food coloring, some metal confetti, then sealing the lid with glue.

FOOD
- Make slushies for the kids by freezing lemonade, then whirling it in the blender and pouring it into paper cups. Give the kids small spoons to eat the slushies with.
- Make Tuna Boats by slicing green peppers in half and filling with a tuna fish, relish, and mayonnaise mixture. Add a cheese triangle for a sail.

FAVORS
- Give the kids squirt guns to take home.
- Let the guests keep their sunglasses.
- Provide the kids with cartoon towels to keep.
- Give the guests sand pails and shovels for the beach.

VARIATIONS
- Take the kids to the beach for a wonderfully Wet and Wild time.

HELPFUL HINTS
- Be sure all the kids can swim and be sure someone is always watching them.

feet from their partner. Give one of the two kids a water balloon. On the word "Go!" the balloon holders are to toss the balloons to their partner. If any pair breaks their balloon, they are out of the game. The rest of the players each take one step back to increase the distance between the pair, then they toss the balloons again. Keep increasing the distance and tossing the balloons until only one pair of players is left.
- Water War: Give everyone a squirt gun and have a water war! You can also use turkey basters, sponges, buckets, hoses, and other water objects.

YO-YO PARTY

Yo! It's a yo-yo party. String along a few friends for a handy afternoon of tricks and stunts with a yo-yo. The kids can "walk the dog," "go around the world," or "rock the cradle"—all with this little toy.

INVITATIONS

- Write the party details with permanent felt-tip pens on yo-yos. Mail in padded envelopes to the guests.
- Cut out yo-yo shapes from construction paper, write the party information on them, attach lengths of string, and mail to the guests.

YO-YO CAKE

1. Make two round cakes and frost them separately with a favorite flavor of icing.
2. Place one cake on a plate and top it with a contrasting color of pudding. For example, if the cake has been frosted white, use chocolate pudding. If the cake has been frosted chocolate, use vanilla or banana pudding.
3. Place the other round cake on top.
4. Wrap a long licorice rope around the cake. Let the end of the rope dangle off the side.
5. Copy a yo-yo inscription onto the top of the cake using tubes of frosting.

COSTUMES

- Ask the kids to attach a yo-yo to themselves in some creative way.
- Have the guests wear athletic clothes.

DECORATIONS

- Hang yo-yos from the trees and fences and set them on the tables around the party room.

- Cut out giant yo-yos from construction paper and use them as decorations and place mats.

GAMES

- Yo-Yo Activities: Get a yo-yo book from the library or bookstore and learn a few tricks to teach the kids. Or get them their own books to use as guides.

- Yo-Yo Doubles: First teach the kids some two-handed yo-yo tricks. Then give them two yo-yos and see what they can do with both hands!

- Yo-Yo Marathons: Line the kids up for a marathon and give each of them a yo-yo. Start the clock and see who can keep their yo-yo going the longest without stopping. Award a prize to the kid who lasts the longest.

- Yo-Yo Olympics: Have each player learn one yo-yo trick from an instruction book, then try to teach everyone else the trick. Give points to the participants based on their ability to perform the new tricks. Add up the points to see who wins the yo-yo Olympics.
- Yo-Yo Relay: Divide the group into teams and line them up. Give the first players a yo-yo and call out a specific trick they must do. The two players race to perform the trick, and as soon as it's completed, they must pass the yo-yo to the next player, who must also do the trick. The team that finishes first wins.

ACTIVITIES

- Yo-Yo Art: Give the kids plain yo-yos when they arrive at the party. Set out paints, felt-tip pens, decals, glitter, puffy paints, and other decorating materials, then let the kids decorate their yo-yos.

VARIATIONS

- Instead of a Yo-Yo Party, host a Jai Alai Party, a Nerf Ball Party, a Jacks-and-Ball Party, a Jump Rope Party, or other game party that uses a prop.

HELPFUL HINTS

- Some of the kids will be more coordinated with the yo-yo than others, so get a few expert yo-yoers to help those at the party who need extra attention.

FOOD

- Offer the kids yo-yo cakes from the bakery section of the grocery store.
- Make cheese-and-cracker yo-yos by using round crackers and round slices of cheese. Sandwich the cheese between the crackers and attach a piece of string cheese.
- Let the kids wash the treats down with cans of Yoo-Hoo.

FAVORS

- Give the kids yo-yos in fancy neon colors.
- Give the kids mini yo-yos.

INDEX

Order Form

Qty.	Title	Author	Order No.	Unit Cost (U.S. $)	Total
	Bad Case of the Giggles	Lansky, B.	2411	$16.00	
	Free Stuff for Kids	Free Stuff Editors	2190	$5.00	
	Girls to the Rescue, Book #1	Lansky, B.	2215	$3.95	
	Girls to the Rescue, Book #2	Lansky, B.	2216	$3.95	
	Girls to the Rescue, Book #3	Lansky, B.	2219	$3.95	
	Girls to the Rescue, Book #4	Lansky, B.	2221	$3.95	
	Girls to the Rescue, Book #5	Lansky, B.	2222	$3.95	
	Girls to the Rescue, Book #6	Lansky, B.	2223	$3.95	
	Happy Birthday to Me!	Lansky, B.	2416	$8.95	
	Kids Are Cookin'	Brown, K.	2440	$8.00	
	Kids' Holiday Fun	Warner, P.	6000	$12.00	
	Kids' Party Cookbook	Warner, P.	2435	$12.00	
	Kids' Party Games and Activities	Warner, P.	6095	$12.00	
	Kids' Pick-A-Party Book	Warner, P.	6090	$9.00	
	Kids Pick the Funniest Poems	Lansky, B.	2410	$16.00	
	Miles of Smiles	Lansky, B.	2412	$16.00	
	New Adventures of Mother Goose	Lansky, B.	2420	$9.95	
	Newfangled Fairy Tales, Book #1	Lansky, B.	2500	$3.95	
	Newfangled Fairy Tales, Book #2	Lansky, B.	2501	$3.95	
	No More Homework! No More Tests!	Lansky, B.	2414	$8.00	
	Poetry Party	Lansky, B.	2430	$12.00	
	Young Marian's Adventures	Mooser, S.	2218	$4.50	
				Subtotal	
			Shipping and Handling (see below)		
			MN residents add 6.5% sales tax		
				Total	

YES! Please send me the books indicated above. Add $2.00 shipping and handling for the first book with a retail price up to $9.99. or $3.00 for the first book with a retail price of over $9.99. Add $1.00 shipping and handling for each additional book. All orders must be prepaid. Most orders are shipped within two days by U.S. Mail (7–9 delivery days). Rush shipping is available for an extra charge. Overseas postage will be billed. **Quantity discounts available upon request.**

Send book(s) to:

Name _____ Address _____

City _____ State _____ Zip _____

Telephone (_____)_____

Payment via:

❑ Check or money order payable to Meadowbrook Press (No cash or COD's please)

❑ Visa (for orders over $10.00 only)   ❑ MasterCard (for orders over $10.00 only)

Account # _____ Signature _____ Exp. Date _____

A *FREE* Meadowbrook Press catalog is available upon request.
You can also phone or fax us with a credit card order.

Mail to: Meadowbrook Press
5451 Smetana Drive, Minnetonka, MN 55343
Toll -Free 1-800-338-2232

Phone (612) 930-1100

Fax (612) 930-1940

For more information (and fun) visit our website:
www.meadowbrookpress.com